FOOD STARS

15 WOMEN STIRRING UP THE FOOD INDUSTRY

ELLEN MAHONEY

WOMEN OF POWER

CHICAGO
REVIEW
PRESS

The Library of Congress has cataloged the hardcover edition under the
following Control Number: 2022940076

Cover and illustrations: Sadie Teper
Interior design: Nord Compo

Printed in the United States of America

Contents

Introduction

Women and food make a dynamic duo.

From finding creative ways for astronauts to eat in space, to operating a 20-acre farm, to fighting for food justice—women are often at the forefront of the enormous food industry that shapes all of our lives.

Each day, women from all over the world bring their families and communities needed nourishment. They work in tall fields of corn, steamy kitchens, or open-air markets. They bring food to breakfast nooks, dining room tables, conference rooms, or even picnic blankets. They work in front of computer screens or film cameras, or in kitchen labs and classrooms chock-full of students.

Women help build important cultural food traditions that are passed down for generations. And if there's not enough accessible and nutritious food for all? It's often women who speak up for change and initiate the problem-solving process.

The 15 women in this book—Emma, Gail, Petra, Caroline, Cheetie, Tracy, Dani, Haleh, Sheila, Andi, Abby, Jocelyn, Takiyah, Sophie, and Pia—have carved out unique paths in their fields. They are hardworking, dedicated, creative, and caring individuals who use their heads, hearts, and hands to shed light on the ever-changing food industry with all its sweet and savory sides.

You'll read about their amazing lives and the important work they do as farmers, chefs, food activists, food storytellers, and food scientists. Each woman has a unique story to tell with plenty of challenges along the way. Most important, they've all found their true passions in life to make a positive difference in our world. And it all revolves around food.

Part I
On the Farm

1

Emma de Long: A Passion for Farming

During the summer of her junior year in high school, Emma de Long set out for the adventure of her life. But the journey was arduous and took 12 hours on a train followed by two long bus rides and a car ride. Her destination was to a remote village along the jade-colored Yalakom River in British Columbia, Canada.

It was the first time Emma had ever traveled by herself, and the village was more than a thousand miles from her California home. Many feelings bubbled up within her. Excitement. Anticipation. Nervousness. The day before she left, her best friend, Rebecca, even cut off her waist-long hair so Emma wouldn't attract unwanted attention on the train.

Emma was motivated. Like many of her friends, Emma was upset with the state of the world and how humans were treating the planet, especially with regard to environmental destruction. She wanted to learn more about farming as a way to feel healthy and happy and to do good work in the world. Emma was determined to learn how to grow her own food and to survive.

When she finally crossed the Canadian border on the train, her eyes were wide as saucers. "Five bald eagles immediately flew by and the mountains rose up and it was just so wild and new to me."

Emma was making this trip as part of the World Wide Opportunities on Organic Farms (WWOOF) program. For free room and board, she would help out on various homesteads for the summer and learn about organic farming along the way. Earlier in the year Emma had looked over a long list of WWOOF farms in Canada. That's when she chose to work in the small village along the Yalakom River. The village was isolated, and families needed to rely on one another for help or to work on projects. There were no cell phones, and the main form of communication was the walkie-talkie. It was a unique community that made sense to her. "It all felt very natural and I thought, 'Oh, this is how I could live.'"

What's a WWOOFer?

According to its mission statement, World Wide Opportunities on Organic Farms (WWOOF) is a "worldwide movement to link visitors with organic farmers, promote a cultural and educational exchange, and build a global community conscious of ecological farming and sustainability practices." The program, originally called Working Weekends on Organic Farms, was founded in England in 1971 by Sue Coppard. Sue was living and working in London at the time and eager to spend more time in the country and volunteer at a farm. Today the international program has sister groups in more than 100 countries. Thousands of organic farmers around the world host volunteers, who are called WWOOFers, to help them gain skills in organic farming and gardening and possibly become a new generation of farmers.

Emma first chose to board with a family that was building a straw-bale house next to a forest. "I really wanted to learn about alternate building methods, and the family had a large vegetable garden and they were making plant medicine. I was interested in all of that."

The family lived in a trailer during their home renovation, and Emma slept in a nearby tepee that had a queen-size bed and a firepit. She thought the tepee was great, but it was situated right next to the woods.

One neighbor quickly warned her, "Don't go into the woods this afternoon. It's all grizzly bears in there."

Emma says she was careful whenever she ventured out. "I was in awe of the woods, but I also definitely felt like a foreigner."

She then moved into a different home with an elderly couple who had a bountiful vegetable garden and an abundance of fruits. Emma would go out every day and pick buckets of raspberries and then spend a lot of time processing the fruit.

The following summer after graduating from high school in 2008, Emma returned to the village to work there once again. She stayed with the same couple as before, but this time she made the journey with Rebecca. "I really fell in love with it up there and enjoyed processing foods and making meals and medicine," Emma says. "Everything that had to do with food was so exciting to me."

Emma de Long is now a farmer and the owner of Kneehigh Farm, located in southeast Pennsylvania. Her farm is completely women-owned and operated and is based on the Community Supported Agriculture (CSA) agricultural method. She and her crew of farmers grow a wide variety of organic vegetables. Her industrious path to becoming a farmer stretches all the way from California to Pennsylvania with many adventures in between.

Community Supported Agriculture

Farmers often love their work, and agriculture is a business where someone can spend quality time outdoors. But there are many environmental factors that can wreak havoc on crops and impact a farmer's earnings.

An innovative way to help farmers have economic stability was developed with Community Supported Agriculture, also called CSA. This method of organic farming ensures that the expenses of running a small farm are offset ahead of time before many plants even begin to sprout. The CSA method connects farmers directly with their community members who buy shares early in the year. This method helps farmers with their ongoing cash flow while offering consumers fresh organic foods throughout the growing season. Every CSA has a different amount of CSA members and fees for their shares. During the growing season CSA members will typically go to the farm on a weekly basis to pick up their items or have them delivered. In addition, CSA farmers often sell produce at local farmers markets. The concept of Community Supported Agriculture has been inspired from countries around the world such as Japan, Switzerland, and the United States.

Emma began her life amid the great outdoors. Born in the coastal town of Santa Cruz, California, she grew up with wilderness and preserved land all around her. The California weather gave her plenty of opportunity to be outside in the fresh air, and the vast Pacific Ocean was just a five-minute bike ride away. She loved to swim in the waves with friends and hang out on the beach after school. Emma was athletic and played soccer her entire childhood, including varsity soccer in high school. "I was always doing a sport like soccer, volleyball, or softball. So being on a team and feeling the capabilities of my body really influenced my love of farming. I was always active and strong."

After high school she took many steps on her road to becoming a full-time farmer, and she often traveled all across the United States to do so. In 2009 she enrolled in a year-long program at the Regenerative Design Institute in Bolinas, California, where she earned a designer's certificate in permaculture. Emma liked the wholistic concepts of permaculture and says it was a mindful approach she wanted to live her life by.

The Art and Science of Permaculture

The term *permaculture* combines the words *permanent*, *agriculture*, and *culture*, and sets forth a philosophy for how humans can live in harmony with nature and grow things in sustainable ways. The term was coined by academics Bill Mollison and David Holmgren during the late 1970s in Australia. However, the science and agricultural methods of permaculture are not new and stem from ancient Indigenous growing techniques: "Its framework is a design system that incorporates core principles and practices from Indigenous knowledge around the world." Permaculture is about observing and mimicking patterns in nature without exploiting nature. David Holmgren introduced 12 design principles of permaculture that cover how to live in sustainable ways and care for our planet. These principles cover topics such as using renewable energy, composting, mulching, saving water, and growing plants vertically.

Over the next few years, Emma headed east and volunteered on various farms to meet new people and learn new skills wherever she landed. Her pay was always room and board. She first worked on the George Jones Farm and Nature Preserve at Oberlin College in Ohio where Rebecca was attending school. She then volunteered at Braddock Farms, which is a small urban farm near Pittsburgh, Pennsylvania.

The years after graduating from high school gave her many unforgettable learning experiences. In 2012 she moved back to California. It was an important moment in her life because it was the first time she was actually paid to farm. She took a job at the eight-acre organic Freewheelin' Farm located on the coast just north of Santa Cruz. The farm provided CSA shares to the Santa Cruz community as well as delivering produce to many of the restaurants in the San Francisco area. During her six-month stay at the farm, Emma lived in a tent near the ocean and could look out over the water every day. Farming on the coast was beautiful, but there were challenges. On windy days Emma had to wear ski googles because the gusts of wind were so strong.

Still, there was always a lot of work to do. She sowed seeds by hand in the greenhouse, weeded the fields, and learned to drive a Kubota Model L245H tractor. "We grew a lot of lettuce, carrots, beets, and potatoes," Emma says. "They were gorgeous high-quality staple crops." Most important, Emma realized that becoming a farmer with a small crew was doable. It was the first time she knew farming could be her full-time career. She was ready for her next big step.

The following year, she moved back to the East Coast to be in the apprenticeship and incubator program at the Seed Farm in Emmaus, Pennsylvania. She enrolled in the Beginning Farmer Program that helps students learn hands-on training in running a farm or agricultural business. After eight months in the program, she developed a business plan that was approved by her instructors and the board members. This success was another defining moment in her life. Her business plan gave her the green light to launch her very first farm on one-and-a-half acres at the Seed Farm.

Emma thought about different names for her farm and eventually decided on Kneehigh Farm. She says the name was a nod to her Santa Cruz roots because the surfing term *knee high* referred to how high the waves were—"knee high to thigh high." The name also incorporated the old farmers' adage, "knee high by the Fourth of July," for measuring a cornstalk's height by Independence Day.

It didn't take long to find her first CSA members, and she began planting her organic vegetable farm in the spring of 2013. She chose a variety of crops including peppers, tomatoes, and eggplants. "Because of the seasons in Pennsylvania, you could grow more than in California," Emma says. "I had a lot of crops the first year."

It was an exciting time in her life, and her younger brother, David, her older sister, Kate, and her parents were right there for her from the start. "My brother came out for a long period of time when I was first farming at the Seed Farm, and Dad would visit for months to help with projects. My sister, who's a pastry chef, brought a fun bubbly energy to the farm."

Two years later, Emma was ready to spread her wings again. She needed more space to grow more food, so she moved Kneehigh Farm about 25 miles south to an area just outside of Pottstown, Pennsylvania. There she rented seven acres and a home from the large 520-acre Lundale Farm, which is home to eight different farmers. "I live in a stone farmhouse that was built in the early 1800s, and I feel really blessed to live here. There's also a greenhouse nearby so I can tend to it in the spring."

As her workload increased, Emma realized she couldn't do everything alone and hired two women to help out part time on the farm. "Once I decided to hire somebody, even part time, it was so motivating. Most people getting involved in farming now are women, and I think women make awesome farmers."

Emma looks for different qualities when hiring a farmer, such as curiosity and a "let's do it" attitude. She feels it's important to be innovative every step of the way and to have a sense of humor. "Farming can be grueling, and you can be covered in mud with boots that weigh 500 pounds. But you can still laugh at it."

She believes women farmers are good at multitasking and finding solutions to problems. "So much of farming is failing and being okay with that. If something is heavy to carry, we have to figure it out. No other person is going to come along and do this for us."

In 2020 when COVID-19 hit, there were plenty of issues for Emma to contend with. "All around us in the food industry we saw so many people suffering. Businesses were closing and there were shortages. There was this crazy scarcity mentality that cropped up, and people worried where they were going to find their food."

When her local community looked to Kneehigh Farm for help, she focused on her CSA members instead of selling wholesale to outside markets. "In a matter of weeks our CSA nearly doubled and buoyed us through the whole year." But because of social distancing and the spread of the corona-virus, some CSA members were reluctant to visit the farm. To help, Emma offered more online ordering and curbside pickup. Her system worked. In 2020 Kneehigh Farm grew 43 different vegetables with 108 varieties for 120 CSA members.

There are many things about farming that Emma loves, such as being in nature every day and seeing the expression on someone's face when they discover what a crop looks like in its natural form. She also never tires of seeing the beautiful fresh flowers that her husband, Aaron, grows on her farm.

But a typical day in the scorching heat of July and August can be a bear. "If it's really hot, I try not to work much past 3:00 PM just because you get exhausted. We try to start earlier and end earlier, but it varies with the weather," she says. "In Pennsylvania the pattern has been wetter summers and more intense late freezes in spring and early freezes in fall. When we have a wet year, it's five inches of rain every week. It drowns everything out. There's no sun. Things don't grow." To deal with these issues, Emma works hard to enrich her soil, which is a big plus for her crops. She also knows from experience that there's always another season.

During Emma's childhood her mom always had plenty of organic food on the table, and it's a big reason why Knee-high Farm's produce is Certified Naturally Grown. "I think the benefits of all the sensations of smell, taste, and touch of real food hits such a primal note in us," she says. "It's what our ancestors have done for generations. It's just not your tongue tasting it—your body feels that it's nourishing you."

In addition to organic food crops, Emma started experimenting with growing indigo and flax on her fields over the past few years. She calls indigo her passion crop. It started when her friend Rebecca took an indigo workshop in Greece and inspired Emma to grow the plant. Emma learned that growing indigo is a complex procedure from harvesting the plant to extracting the pigment, which is primarily used to dye cotton yarn a blue color. "You can't just take the pigment and put it into water and dye something. You have to create this whole very witchy chemistry," she laughs.

Growing flax, which is used to create linen, had unexpected results and lifted her spirits during the tough times of COVID-19. "We seeded late April and it started blooming by the end of June. The blue flowers of the plants looked like these waves of water undulating in the wind. It was breathtaking."

Emma is a first-generation farmer, and she's learned through many years of hard work, preparation, and study that it's not for everyone. But it's definitely for some. "I feel like farmers are so innovative," she says. "Sharing food and sharing a meal is something so primitive, and it just hits something in all of us where we feel, *Yes, I'm human and I'm part of this Earth. I want to take care of this Earth.* So farming really ties in full circle for me, and I would never change my life for another path."

Emma's Favorites

Time of day: I like the early morning before the wind picks up and when the light is still lazy and everything is waking.

Time of year: Autumn, because of a shifting of energy, from constant heat and work, to slow days and a rekindling of relaxed, cozy kitchen time. My birthday is in October and is a strong time to reflect on birth and renewal.

Food: I love to grow and eat winter squash, especially delicata. I love to see how quickly they sprawl out and

I love a heavy harvest. I enjoy experimenting with them in the kitchen, or just cutting them in half and roasting for a quick side dish. The warming, sweet reminder that these came from the ground and will feed me for many months is a welcome reflection after the long, hard days of summer.

Saying: My grandma used to say, "There are no mistakes, just adjustments and corrections." I hold this dear to my heart.

Mentor: I admire my mother and I am learning why more deeply each year.

Movie: *Anne of Green Gables* (1985).

Book: *East of Eden* by John Steinbeck.

Follow Emma de Long Online

Website: kneehighfarm.com

Instagram: @kneehighfarm

Facebook: @kneehighfarmCSA

Gail Taylor: Urban Farmer

When Gail Taylor decided to start a farm in the Washington, DC, area, there were all sorts of challenges ahead. First of all, it wasn't easy to find the land that was available for farming she needed in DC. And once she found the land and a willing landlord, Gail was suddenly faced with navigating very high property taxes. This took her to the DC City Council, where she met with policy makers to fight for urban farmers. After years of hard work, her efforts paid off and her dreams of farming became a reality.

And then when it was time to name her new farm, she quickly came up with something that hit all the right notes: Three Part Harmony Farm.

"Three-part harmony" was an expression her dad used frequently when she was growing up, and it's been a meaningful concept throughout her life. "It's when people get together and have to do something as a group that they haven't done before," Gail says. "And then all of a sudden without even practicing, everyone is singing their part. We're all contributing to a project, and it becomes this beautiful, melodious thing."

Gail could easily see how operating her farm with her team required working together and figuring things out along the way to create something harmonious. In her case it wasn't creating a playlist of songs, it was growing and harvesting a wide variety of vegetables and herbs.

Gail Taylor is an urban farmer and the owner of Three Part Harmony Farm, a Community Supported Agriculture (CSA) farm in the heart of Washington, DC. She's been farming since 2005, but her career hasn't always been focused on growing organic foods for her community. Gail has a degree in political science from Syracuse University in New York, with an emphasis on US foreign policy in Latin America.

Urban Farming

Unlike agriculture that takes places in a rural farm setting, urban farming occurs in or near a city. An urban farm can seem like an unlikely oasis and a breath of fresh air in the concrete world of a city. These farms are a vital means for providing nutritious and accessible food for the community.

Urban farmers find many unique places to grow organic food. How about a plot of land near a business, school, church, freeway off-ramp, or even a front yard or rooftop? With some hardy soil and resilient seedlings, farmers can turn these urban areas into viable farms overflowing with crops.

This type of farming is not a new concept. During World War I and World War II, victory gardens, also called war gardens, were grown in cities to provide much-needed nutritious food during wartime when essential food items were being rationed. In recent years many people have grown gardens in home or urban settings during the COVID-19 pandemic.

Urban farms are often Community Supported Agriculture (CSA) models, and customers prepay for food shares throughout the year. These farms also help community members learn more about how food is grown and where it comes from.

Gail was born in Rock Island, Illinois, which is located on the Mississippi River on the western side of the state. Rock Island is known for the historic railroad bridge that was completed in 1856. This railway bridge was the first to cross the Mississippi River, allowing train passengers to now travel from Illinois to Iowa and beyond.

She grew up with two younger brothers in a large extended family. Her paternal grandfather's family were sharecroppers from Mississippi and picked cotton for a living. When her grandfather was in his twenties, he decided to find work in the railroad industry. He moved from Mississippi and traveled hundreds of miles north to Rock Island during a key time in America called the Great Migration. During the Great Migration, which lasted from 1916 to 1970, more than six million Black Americans moved from southern states to northern, midwestern, and western states in search of better work opportunities and living conditions.

Gail had an active childhood in Rock Island and remembers playing team sports, such as soccer and softball. But she sometimes felt isolated. "We lived in the middle of nowhere, and we were surrounded by farms and cornfields. My whole life was with friends in the neighborhood and going to school."

Her mom had a small vegetable garden in the backyard, and Gail had a flower garden on one side of her house where she grew marigolds. She remembers carefully counting out 100 tiny marigold seeds and bringing them to school for a class assignment to celebrate the 100th day of school.

Gail's home was always overflowing with music, which created many song-filled memories. "Music is an incredibly important part of my life," she says. "My dad is a singer-songwriter, and I have fond memories of him coming home from work in the evenings and immediately sitting down at the piano."

And many of her relatives sang in church choirs. "I grew up around any kind of music or instrument you can think of that would be in a church. I can also sing along to just about every song from the mid-'80s to the mid-'90s performed by female singers or all-girl groups. That's my coming-of-age era."

When Gail was a teen, her family moved to the Albany, New York, area. After graduating from high school, Gail attended Syracuse University in Syracuse, New York, and earned a degree in political science with an emphasis on Latin America, social justice, and foreign policy. "I liked history and politics and wanted to be a career foreign service officer. I studied Spanish in school and learning about Latin America seemed like it would open more opportunities for travel."

Her first job out of college took her to Capitol Hill in Washington, DC, when she was 21. Surrounded by a high-energy community of politicians and lawmakers amid many museums and historic monuments, she landed her first job during the summer of 1999. "I worked as a political organizer on a political prisoner campaign, which was connected to the Latin America Solidarity Movement."

Gail also volunteered on affordable-housing campaigns in the District of Columbia. It was a vibrant time in her life, but after working five years in DC, she experienced what she calls her "quarter-life crisis." Now in her mid-20s, she felt unfulfilled by political work and grassroots lobbying. "I didn't want to go to work and just turn on a computer. I wanted a job that was more tangible."

Gail knew her career needed a major reboot and she was ready to do something else. Little did she know she was about to experience three major life changes over the next ten years. It would be an amazing three-part journey.

Her first major change meant moving to Guatemala in 2004. Fluent in Spanish, Gail began volunteering for a nongovernmental organization called Puente de Paz (Peace Bridge) to interview Guatemalan women and document their heart-rending stories related to the Guatemalan Civil War. She also assisted the staff at Puente de Paz when they gave monthly classes about natural health techniques and herbal medicines.

After six months in Central America, followed by a trip to Germany, Gail returned to DC to begin her second major life change. At this pivotal point in her life, she hung up her power suit and put on jeans, a T-shirt, boots, and a hat. She wanted to be out in nature and farm.

In the fall of 2005, Gail began volunteering at the 285-acre Clagett Farm, a CSA in Maryland, which was a 45-minute drive from her home. "I started volunteering at this farm because I was interested in learning about where my food came from and having a healthy lifestyle."

Her interest in food began in earnest after attending many funerals when she was a teen and seeing loved ones die from diseases related to unhealthy diets. "I read that having a plant-based diet was healthy, so it seemed like something to do." She tried vegetarianism for a short time as a preteen and then gradually starting eating less meat during high school.

"When I went to college, my freshman roommate was a vegetarian and so then I finally went cold turkey," Gail laughs.

Gail remembers her first season at Clagett because it was very rainy and she was often outside for the entire day. But it was a good feeling that took her back to her childhood days of playing soccer with her brothers. "We would be drenched from playing soccer on a rainy Saturday and my mom would take us home and put all our clothes in the dryer. Then we'd go back to the soccer field for the next siblings' match!"

During the next five years at Clagett, Gail dug in and learned the ropes of farming. She figured out everything from growing and planting seedlings, to weeding, harvesting crops, and organizing a CSA. Gail eventually became a senior member of the crew and supported the vegetable operations manager in maintaining 20 acres of vegetable crops on the farm. Farming suited her, and she began to enjoy her work more and see the fruits of her labor. She says it was like putting on a slipper that fit.

"I loved that I could start the morning weeding and at lunchtime stand up and look behind me and see what I had accomplished. And on Saturday when 200 families would come with their children and pick up the food we had grown, that made me really content and happy."

In addition, Gail also worked part-time at the Maryland University Food Co-op, a worker-owned collective. She volunteered there for years in exchange for store credit. The co-op's motto was "Food for people, not for profit."

What Is Food Security?

The term *food security* has to do with people having access to obtain and consume nutritious food for health. "Food security, as defined by the United Nations' Committee on World Food Security, means that all people, at all times, have physical, social, and economic access to sufficient, safe, and nutritious food that meets their food preferences and dietary needs for an active and healthy life." Factors that block people from having food security include things such as a community's lack of available and affordable healthy and fresh food.

In 2011 it was time for change again, and this one would be monumental. Gail was eager and ready to start her own farm in DC. But she knew it wasn't going to be easy. Finding farmland in the hubbub of the District of Columbia would be tricky.

She put her math and organizing skills to work and wrote a business plan for how her farm would look. She thought about the crops she would grow, the people who could work at her farm, and how her farm would contribute to the community. She then created a spreadsheet of possible land parcels in the DC area and searched high and low throughout the city.

Gail finally found a two-acre grass field behind the main building of an order of Catholic priests called the Missionary Oblates of Mary Immaculate. The field was in the Brookland neighborhood of DC and about three-and-a-half miles from the White House. It was rarely used except for the occasional soccer game.

Gail says she cold called the order's head priest, Father Séamus P. Finn, to set up a meeting to discuss her visions for a farm. "As soon as he sat down in the conference room, he was, and to this day, remains my number one supporter and advocate."

Father Séamus was onboard for Gail to transition their two-acre field into a small urban farm. But it wasn't easy-breezy, because the field was designated for nonprofit use only. The priests were concerned about the tax implications related to using the field for a commercial business—like Gail's small urban farm. In fact, it would cost the hefty tax fee of about $50,000 a year. "That's a whole lot of cucumbers!" Gail says, not knowing whether to laugh or cry.

But the money matter didn't stop her. She believed the two-acre field would be ideal for her farm, and she was ready to fight for it. Gail tapped into her background in politics and advocacy work. She quickly learned that many US farmers have an agriculture exemption and are exempt from paying full property taxes for their farmland. Gail wondered if she could also receive a tax break if the oblate's field could be considered farmland. But because the District of Columbia is not a state of the United States and does not have a Department of Agriculture, it seemed like Gail was out of luck.

Determined, she still wasn't ready to give up. "I went back to my political organizing days and resuscitated all of that skill set and started building and amassing a group of people who were working on the issue together. It was a long, multistep thing."

Gail turned to her local city council and American University's law clinic for help. She then started working with DC council members David Grosso and Mary Cheh to draw up a bill that would change and improve tax regulations for DC urban farmers. But it didn't happen overnight.

For the next three years, Gail worked with the council members and AU law student volunteers on the I Want DC to Grow campaign, which was designed to support her goals and help other urban farmers in the area.

During the long legislative process as the bill was being finalized, Gail supported herself by managing a yoga studio and selling seedlings grown in her backyard. In 2012 the oblates signed a lease directly with Gail that allowed her to begin farming on the two-acre field as long as she donated her crops to charities and individuals in the DC community. It gave her time to enrich the field's soil, which was severely depleted of nutrients, to grow crops, and to enlist volunteers to help out at the fledgling Three Part Harmony Farm.

Finally, in 2014, the city council passed the DC Urban Farming and Food Security Act of 2014. This bill, often referred to as the DC Farm Bill, helped Gail with a full tax break and paved the way for future urban farmers in the DC metropolitan area. She could now operate her farm and sell produce.

Today Gail grows many greens such as lettuce, collard greens, and swiss chard, along with a wide assortment of vegetables and herbs. She uses sustainable farming practices with no chemical pesticides or herbicides.

Following the CSA model, Gail signs up members early in the season who pay in advance to pick up weekly shares throughout the year. She typically hires two to three crew members to help harvest from May to November each year.

Although Gail loves to farm, she has experienced hard times along the way. She says it's challenging for farmers to run small organic farms and be economically successful. Since the beginning, Gail has supplemented her farm work with other income such as working at the Maryland food co-op and the yoga studio. And since 2019, Gail has been the conference manager of the Future Harvest annual conference of the Chesapeake Alliance for Sustainable Agriculture.

She also says that as a Black woman, doors have been closed to her. "I don't have access to go to lucrative farmers markets, and I made a decision a couple of years ago to completely drop out of the farmers market scene." Instead, she delivers her CSA shares at a local hardware store that's close to her farm.

An important part of her life is being part of the Black Dirt Farm Collective, a close-knit group of Black farmers in surrounding states. "We're like family," Gail says. In the collective she does volunteer work such as organizing Afro-ecology events. The collective maintains memberships and supports food sovereignty in the National Black Food and Justice Alliance and the Climate Justice Alliance.

From political organizer to urban farmer, Gail cares deeply about her mission to provide healthy food for her community. Her logo for Three Part Harmony Farm is a beautiful monarch butterfly known for its migratory journeys between Mexico and the United States. The monarch represents so much for her. "Young Black farmers of my generation who don't grow up in farming families must make an intentional decision to come back to the land," Gail says. "We are the Return Generation, smaller in number but equally determined to find dignity in our search for nourishing food while at the same time being able to pay for the roof over our heads."

Gail's Favorites

Time of day: I love the sunset, especially if I'm at the farm. If I'm working while the sun is setting, I'm most likely by myself. It's a special "me time" when I do tasks by myself, most often because I'm finishing up whatever the crew wasn't able to do that day or even that week.

Time of year: I love the late winter/early springtime when the greenhouse chores are in full swing. There's just something so satisfying and rewarding when you watch seeds germinate and then grow into strong, healthy plants that then get planted out at the farm.

Place on Earth: My mom's kitchen.

Food to grow: Greens!

Food to eat: Greens!

Songs: I like almost anything from a Motown Greatest Hits album. I love all Aretha Franklin music, especially "Respect." I like "Lovely Day," and other great songs by Bill Withers.

Motto: Three Part Harmony Farm's motto is, "Food as Medicine. Food as Culture. Food for Our Future."

Books: Two books that were incredibly influential for me at the time that I was on the verge of beginning a process of politicization are *Open Veins of Latin America* by Eduardo Galeano, and *Lies My Teacher Told Me* by James W. Loewen.

Follow Gail Taylor Online

Website: threepartharmonyfarm.org

Instagram: @3phfarm

Twitter: @3PHarmony

Facebook: @threepartharmony

Petra Page-Mann: Sowing Seeds

Petra Page-Mann is a one-of-a-kind trailblazer. Literally. During her high school summers she worked for the Adirondack Mountain Club and built trails throughout the lake-filled forest region of the Adirondacks. "I would be in the mountains building trails all day long," she says. "It was amazing."

The Adirondack Mountains are a scenic and protected area of the United States that cover thousands of miles of wilderness in northeastern New York State. Its large network of trails, some of which Petra helped build, enables people to enjoy sports such as backpacking, camping, fishing, and skiing. Well-known individuals from all over the world have visited this unique area for hundreds of years. In the summer of 1858, poet Ralph Waldo Emerson traveled to the Adirondacks to write poetry while he stayed in a rustic setting dubbed the Philosopher's Camp.

After graduating from high school in 2002, Petra joined the AmeriCorps National Civilian Community Corps (NCCC) for one year and headed out west to work in Colorado. Founded in 1993, the AmeriCorps is a volunteer community service program that works with local, state, and national organizations throughout the United States.

It took courage for her to leave home and personal strength to fulfill the challenging physical labor that awaited her. Petra was recruited to work with the Colorado Fourteeners Initiative, and her job was to build and preserve trails at 12,000 to 14,000 feet (3,700 to 4,300 m) above sea level where the air is thin, the vegetation is sparse, and one's lifestyle is basically off the grid.

Her job was to work in the Yankee Boy Basin, which is located in the San Juan Mountains of southwest Colorado, not far from the ski town of Telluride. "It was so dreamy up there. I helped build the Mt. Sneffels trail, which didn't exist before. It was super fun."

Along with the other volunteers, Petra would backpack in all her food and set up camp at tree line for weeks at a time. Although the mountaintop views were breathtaking, her diet of highly processed cheddar cheese and crackers definitely fell short. "A dichotomy started to happen for me where I realized I wanted to be in the wildest of places, but that meant I was subject to eating the most industrialized food on the planet.

That's when I realized that farming could be this intersection of all these passions I have—food, being outside and getting dirty, and just being engaged with the world around me."

An important seed had been planted in Petra's mind at this time that would forever influence her life.

Petra Page-Mann is a farmer, writer, musician, and the co-owner of Fruition Seeds, a certified organic seed farm in the village of Naples, New York. Fruition Seeds sells organic, regionally adapted vegetable, flower, and herb seeds for the Northeast. Petra runs the farm with Matthew Goldfarb, whom she calls her "partner in life, love, and all of the above."

Petra grew up in what's called the Finger Lakes region of the northwest area of New York State. From a satellite view, 11 elongated fingerlike lakes define this scenic area that's known for its wineries, boating, fishing, and winter sports.

During her childhood, Petra's family lived in a cozy old farmhouse in Naples. Her home was just a five-minute drive to the 16-mile-long Canandaigua Lake, which is the fourth-largest Finger Lake. Her family didn't farm, but her father had a large garden in their backyard that Petra says was a "huge, beautiful universe." This is where she first learned about saving the seeds of tomatoes, beans, and peas.

"I was immersed in this world of sowing seeds and harvesting, and we were always saving seeds." Petra says she'll always be grateful for her family garden. "All my love of growing things definitely comes straight from my father."

A great deal of Petra's childhood was spent playing outdoors with her younger sister, Greta, and roaming the thousands of acres of forest adjacent to her home where she liked to track minks or hunt for salamanders. During warmer months, Petra's mother would create elaborate scavenger hunts for her daughters. "She would send us out with these lists to find a white or red oak acorn, a metamorphic or sedimentary rock, a blue jay feather, or a jawbone. Our mother taught us to pay attention to nature in these really epic ways."

Petra also loved to write as a child, and she created many small books with her own stories and illustrations. "My mother kept dozens of these little books that I made."

After working in the AmeriCorps program as a teen, she wanted to learn more about the world and spent the next six months traveling by herself throughout Central America. She visited countries such as Costa Rica and Guatemala and trekked around national parks and climbed volcanoes. With only about a thousand dollars to live on, Petra worked on different organic farms from time to time. "I fell in love with the food and culture there, and I got to see another side of agriculture and humanity. I kept getting deeper and deeper into farming."

When Petra moved back to the United States, it was time to regroup and figure out what she wanted to do next. "I'm a really big dreamer and not a list maker in the typical type A sense. But I made this huge list of all the things that I wanted to learn about, from beekeeping to basketmaking to seed saving."

She also made a list of all the skills she wanted to learn and integrate into her life over the years ahead.

Her next adventure took her to Maine, the easternmost state in the United States. There Petra worked for one season at the Mandala Farm, a CSA organic farm in the coastal fishing town of Gouldsboro. Petra was fascinated with this particular farm because the owners used Fjord horses instead of tractors to plow the fields. During her stay at Mandala, she lived in a small cabin in the woods right on Gouldsboro Bay.

"Mandala had all these things I wanted to learn about. They had three acres of vegetables and two acres of orchards. They also had one milk cow, two beef cows, cashmere goats, and broiler and laying hens. I thought it was awesome." Petra says she wanted to immerse herself on a farm that had crops as well as animals to learn more about the fundamentals of how ecosystems work.

She was also rethinking the foods she ate. "I was raised predominantly vegetarian and I was vegan for four years. And then I came to this purely intellectual revelation that nutrient cycling doesn't happen without animals. Mandala was a perfect introduction to that."

From the East Coast, she then traveled cross-country to the Pacific Northwest to work on different farms from British Columbia to Oregon. When she landed in Williams, Oregon, which is in the southern part of the state, she began working at the Seven Seeds Farm. The job turned out to be an important experience for her because she learned about starting a seed company from the ground up.

Seven Seeds is the family farm stewarded by Don Tipping and Stacey Denton. It's also home to Siskiyou Seeds, a certified organic seed company that works with a number of regional seed producers in Oregon and surrounding states. "Don Tipping is an amazing seed grower and permaculture guru," Petra says. "I'm really grateful that I got to be a part of Don Tipping's initial formulation of Siskiyou Seeds so that I could imagine what it was like myself."

After living in Oregon for four years, and working at Seven Seeds Farm for two years, Petra traveled back to the Finger Lakes region in 2011 and was hired by the large international Bejo Seeds company, which breeds both organic and conventional seeds for growers. "There are seed growers, seed breeders, and seed distributors," Petra says. "Bejo is a plant breeding company and sells their seeds to distributors." She worked as the company's trials manager for New York for one year, and the focus of her work was predominantly on cabbage, onion, and carrot seeds.

Sow What?

Almost everything we eat starts with a seed. "Their tininess contains everything an embryonic plant needs to grow into the head of lettuce, abundant arnica, or a giant sequoia." But it's common to forget about these small energetic forces of nature that are either obvious or hidden in foods. While a strawberry is speckled with many tiny seeds on its outside, the large avocado seed boldly sits inside the fruit.

It's helpful to recognize the different types of seeds that farmers or gardeners sow.

Open-pollinated seeds produce plants that are similar to the original parent plants. Two similar plants are pollinated.

Heirloom seeds come from two similar parent plants that are open-pollinated and passed down through generations. These seeds are at least 50 years old and can be saved and reused to produce similar plants.

Cross-pollinated seeds, also called hybrid seeds, will produce plants that have different traits from the original parent plants. Two different plants are pollinated. (Seeds can be reused but will not produce similar plants.)

Organic seeds produce plants that have been grown organically (without synthetic pesticides, herbicides, or fertilizers) and meet organic certification standards.

Regionally adapted seeds, also called local seeds, are seeds that produce plants that have a better chance of growing in specific regions of a state or country.

Genetically Modified Organism (GMO) seeds are created in a lab where the basic genetic material of the seed is altered.

For nearly ten years before starting Fruition Seeds, Petra gained an invaluable understanding of farming and how seed companies operate—from the smallest organic seed grower to a large agribusiness. But she dreamed of starting her own seed company.

Her dream became a reality on an Ithaca, New York, dance floor when Petra met Matthew Goldfarb for the first time during a swing dance. "We both love to dance!" she exclaimed.

Wanting to get to know Matthew that evening, Petra asked him an important question: "What do you love?" He immediately told her he loved blue whales and farming, which caught Petra's attention. But when Matthew mentioned he had grown up with Brian Campbell who cofounded Uprising Seeds with his wife, Crystine Goldberg, Petra was hooked. "They are huge mentors of mine," she says. "So within 30 seconds we were talking about seeds, and within two weeks we were seriously talking about starting a seed company. Nine months later we signed our LLC papers to start Fruition Seeds in 2012."

That year, Petra and Matthew began a Kickstarter campaign to bring in seed money. They then leased a few acres in Naples from a local farmer and planted their first crops of zucchinis, cucumbers, lettuce, and flowers. "We grew the core of what we knew we could grow well and what people would be interested in," Petra says.

Every January they celebrate Coming to Fruition Day to honor the beginning of their seed farm.

Saving Seeds

Farmers and gardeners use saved seeds for the plants they will ultimately plant and grow. Seeds can be saved from fruits, vegetables, grains, herbs, and flowers, and saving open-pollinated seeds will most likely yield plants that resemble the genetic makeup of the parent plant. Seeds come in many different shapes and sizes and are considered either wet or dry when they're harvested.

Wet seeds come from fleshy and often juicy foods such as tomatoes, cucumbers, watermelons, peppers, eggplant, pumpkins, and squash, and are embedded inside the food. The process of extracting seeds means scooping out the seeds from the food's interior, soaking the seeds in water for a few days to ferment them so they grow better, separating the seeds from the fruit pulp after fermentation, and then washing, drying, and storing the seeds.

Dry seeds come from foods such as peas, beans, lettuce, cabbage, broccoli, corn, onions, and flowers (like sunflowers). Dry seeds are found on the outside of the plant in a dried brown pod or seed head. For example, legume seeds are harvested from pods that have dried out. Lettuce grows a flower stalk that shoots up and produces a seed head in a process called bolting. Dry seeds can be obtained by plucking them off or scraping them from plants that have gone to seed and are dry.

With legumes, the dried pods can be cracked open and the seeds pulled out. With corn, the dry corn kernels are pulled or shucked off the cob.

Before planting, wet or dry seeds must be stored and kept dry, cool, and in a dark place in labeled containers such as glass jars or paper bags.

In the beginning, Petra and Matthew did all the farming themselves with a lot of help from friends who volunteered. There were also growing pains. During the initial months of their fledgling business, Petra was excited to create their first crop plan. But after crunching the numbers to see how much seed they could grow and how many seed packets they could sell, she had a grim realization. "I announced to Matthew that there was no way we were ever going to make a living just growing all the seeds ourselves and only having those seeds to share."

Over time they realized that going it alone wasn't going to bring in enough money. "That's when we realized we can support and collaborate with other farms and get seeds from them," Petra says.

Today, their team of seven additional full-time employees (as of 2020) grows 60 percent of their seeds, and the other 40 percent of the seeds comes from collaborating with various organic farms in New York, such as the Remembrance Farm. The result is more than 300 varieties of organic, non–genetically modified, and open-pollinated seeds that are meant for farming in the Northeast. Their seeds are sold via their website in colorful Fruition Seeds packets.

Petra and Matthew now own 20 acres in Naples and farm between four to six acres for seed production. The balance of the land is used to build soil via regenerative cover crops. They had originally leased this land for eight years before buying it from a fifth-generation farmer in 2020.

In addition to farming, Petra also writes and produces many how-to pieces to accompany the crops they grow through the Fruition Seeds website and social media. Her informational pieces are enhanced with many photographs and describe the history and background of plants, as well as the best time to sow, harvest, and save their seeds. In addition, Petra writes educational blog posts for the Cornell College of Agriculture and Life Sciences Small Farms program. She also wrote the book *Rise & Shine: Starting Seeds with Ease* to help readers learn more about growing food and starting seeds.

Over the years, Petra and Matthew have attended various flower shows throughout the Northeast to promote and sell their seeds. For many years, they've set up a booth at the Philadelphia Garden Show in Philadelphia, Pennsylvania, to sell their seeds on a large eye-catching display wall. The garden show comes to life in the city's convention center and draws thousands of visitors to its magical and fragrant world. "There's nothing quite like it and it's very surreal," Petra says. "Imagine 30-foot flowering magnolias that have been brought inside and thousands of daffodils, tulips, and hyacinths covered up with mulch so it looks like a landscape. What makes this flower show so exceptional is that they always have a theme." She adds that her favorite theme was the 2016 Explore America centennial celebration of national parks.

So many factors have played a role in Petra's dream of starting a seed farm: saving seeds in her father's garden, her love of the outdoors and feeling at one with nature, looking for hidden delights on her scavenger hunts as a child, eating healthy food, her fortitude for physical labor, learning about farming all across the United States as well as in Central America and Canada—and meeting Matthew. She has made a vibrant life and career for herself focused on seeds—from the smallest snapdragon seed she compares to dust to her largest seed, the scarlet runner bean. She often says, "Sow seeds and sing songs," and visitors to her farm may sometimes hear her playing the clarinet or accordion in the fields.

"Seeds are stories and we are stories," Petra says. "Seeds are living links in this long line of everything that has been and everything that will be. They're just these beautiful love letters from the past."

Petra's Favorites

Time of day: Early dawn when the stars are fading and birds start singing.

Time of year: Each day is my favorite.

Seeds to grow: Radicchio and dahlias.

Food: Anything lacto-fermented.

Song: "Would You Harbor Me" by Sweet Honey in the Rock.

Saying: "If you have come here to help me you are wasting your time, but if you have come because your liberation is bound up with mine, then let us work together." —Lilla Watson

Mentor: Don Tipping, steward of Siskiyou Seeds.

Movie: *Saving Mr. Banks.*

Book: *Winners Take All: The Elite Charade of Changing the World* by Anand Giridharadas.

Follow Petra Page-Mann Online

Website: fruitionseeds.com

Instagram: @fruition_seeds

Facebook: Fruition Seeds

YouTube: Fruition Seeds

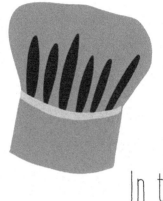

Part II
In the Kitchen

Caroline Glover:
Award-Winning Chef

While growing up in a small town in Texas, Caroline Glover had an active life and spent a great deal of time playing basketball and running track. But after her sophomore year of college, she hit a wall that almost seemed insurmountable. For starters, her major in nutrition didn't feel like a good fit anymore. And on top of everything, Caroline was struggling with an eating disorder she'd had for nearly three years. "I sat down with my parents and just said, 'I'm so unhappy and I don't want to do this anymore.'"

Caroline needed to rethink where her life was going and what she wanted to do next. After a lot of soul searching, she decided to leave college and attend culinary school where she could follow her passion for cooking.

Over the next ten years, Caroline moved away from home, became an excellent cook, worked in a number of top-notch restaurants, started to farm, and then eventually opened her own restaurant. It was a vibrant life-awakening journey that took her from Texas to California, and then on to New York, Pennsylvania, Vermont, and Colorado.

And best of all? This new direction was a lot more on track with her life goals.

Caroline Glover is the chef and owner of Annette in Aurora, Colorado. Since 2017, she has earned many prestigious awards for her cooking. In 2020 she was a James Beard Award finalist in the Best Chef, Mountain category. Caroline has also been a James Beard semifinalist in the Best Chef, Mountain; Best Chef, Southwest; and the Best New Restaurant categories. In 2019 she was named one of the Food and Wine Best New Chefs in America, by *Food and Wine* magazine.

Who Is James Beard?

Born in 1903 in Portland, Oregon, James Beard was an iconic and acclaimed pioneer in the world of American food. He was first drawn to theater and acting during his early career.

But by his mid-30s, his interests turned to food and in 1937 he started a catering company in New York City called Hors d'Oeuvre, Inc. This interest in catering led to the publication of his first cookbook, *James Beard's Hors d'Oeuvre and Canapes*, published in 1940. A later edition featured an introductory note by his good friend and culinary colleague, Julia Child. Beard continued to write more than 20 cookbooks. When he was in his 40s, Beard hosted the live NBC television show called *I Love to Eat*. It was the first TV cooking show in the United States and aired for about nine months. In 1955 he opened the James Beard Cooking School that had locations in New York and Oregon. The James Beard Foundation was founded in 1986, about one year after Beard's death, to honor his life and work. Each year the foundation honors the creative work of a diverse range of American culinary professionals and food leaders with the James Beard Awards.

Caroline grew up in College Station, Texas—a college town on the eastern side of the Lone Star State. Her home was just minutes away from Texas A&M University. She grew up with an older brother, Charles, and a younger sister, Alli, and she remembers enduring many hot and humid days in her hometown. Countless hours were spent swimming in backyard pools or jumping through lawn sprinklers with neighborhood friends.

Caroline says her mom was a great cook, and she especially loved to make jam. She would take her daughters to orchards in rural parts of town to pick blueberries, dewberries, and pecans for mouthwatering jams and pies. Although Caroline wasn't gung ho about foraging as a child, she remembers that time in her life vividly. "I really cherish those memories now."

One summer, she and Alli started a cooking and baking school in their kitchen for neighborhood kids. "It was all sugar," Caroline laughs.

But during her teens Caroline says that food didn't interest her and for the most part she didn't want much to do with it. At 15 she began undereating and became quite thin. Caroline says her basketball coaches noticed how underweight she looked during her senior year of high school. "They were like, 'You're just too skinny. You can play but you need to bulk up,'" she says. But Caroline wasn't ready. "No way, I thought. I'm not going to do that." And she quit playing on the team.

Her family also noticed her weight loss. "My mom took me to a nutritionist, and at some point the nutritionist looked at me and basically said, 'She's all right.'"

Wanting to feel better and learn more about food, Caroline became a nutrition major at Texas Christian University in Dallas–Fort Worth. "I was trying to figure out how to eat," she explains.

But after her freshman and sophomore years, Caroline realized that TCU wasn't working out for her on many levels. The science courses in nutrition weren't her cup of tea, and she didn't connect with many of the other students. Most of all she wanted to redirect her studies and learn how to cook.

"I was super into the Food Network when Rachael Ray was getting big."

And that's when she let her parents know she wanted to change schools and start over. This meant applying to a culinary school.

Caroline was quickly accepted at the Culinary Institute of America in Hyde Park, New York, located on the Hudson River about an hour and a half north of New York City. She visited the school with her dad but was nervous about taking this leap. Her father helped her get over understandable jitters. "My dad's my number one cheerleader," she says. "Anytime I was scared to do something, he was like, 'Yes, let's do it!'"

However, there was one culinary caveat. Caroline needed to work in a kitchen for at least six months before starting at the institute. With the help of her dad, she looked into work opportunities in Yosemite National Park in California and decided to find a job there. Her family had gone backpacking earlier that summer in Yosemite, and Caroline loved being near the towering sequoia trees, waterfalls, valley meadows, mountain vistas, and wildlife. "It was the most at peace I'd felt in a really long time."

Her parents were supportive of her wishes and she quickly got a job at the historic and legendary Ahwahnee Hotel in Yosemite. She started off in the kitchen's enormous pantry station making cold dishes such as salads and sandwiches.

When she wasn't at work, she lived in an employee tent near the hotel, which she really liked. "You're in this pristine place," she says. "You wake up and you can see Half Dome." Half Dome is one of the most world-renowned rock formations in Yosemite.

Caroline liked being around a diverse, fun-loving group of new friends in an environment that was so different from her conservative upbringing in Texas. "I really fell in love with the kitchen culture and food there. But I fell way more in love with the people working in the kitchen. It was like, 'This is where I want to be.'"

After about nine months at the Ahwahnee Hotel, Caroline drove cross-country to begin school at the Culinary Institute of America. During the two-year program at the school, she had classroom lectures in the morning and cooking classes in the afternoon. She also needed to follow strict uniform requirements for the kitchen. She wore black-and-white checkered chef pants, a chef coat, a cravat neckerchief, an apron, and the tall white chef hat called a toque.

"It was a pretty intense, rigorous program," Caroline says. "You had to work hard, but I just took to it. I wanted to be the best."

The Kitchen Brigade

Commercial kitchens have an organizational system called the kitchen brigade developed in the late 1800s by the famous French chef Georges August Escoffier. Working as a chef in a kitchen is a physically and mentally demanding position that is often fast-paced over long hours. It takes organized teamwork. And because kitchen space can be tight, chefs need to be able to move around efficiently without bumping into one another. The modern-day kitchen brigade system includes a variety of chefs with different titles and responsibilities such as:

Executive chef: Manages the business aspects of the kitchen.

Head chef: First in command in the kitchen. The head chef creates menus, manages the kitchen brigade, purchases food, and plates food.

Sous-chef: As second in charge, the sous-chef (*sous* is pronounced SU) often has similar responsibilities to the head chef. The French word *sous* means "under." The sous-chef oversees food preparation.

Chef de partie: Also known as a line cook, or station chef, this individual works in various cold and hot kitchen stations. The French word *partie* means "part."

Commis chef: The *commis* (pronounced co-ME) chef is a junior chef. Duties include jobs such as peeling potatoes, cutting onions, washing spinach, cooking vegetables, and chopping herbs. The French word *commis* means "assistant" or "clerk."

When Caroline graduated from the Culinary Institute of America in 2008, she landed her first job at the acclaimed Spotted Pig restaurant in New York City. The restaurant, which served high-end tavern-style dishes such as chargrill burgers with Roquefort cheese, oysters with mignonette, frittatas, and flourless chocolate cake, was awarded one Michelin Star from 2006 to 2016.

The Michelin Star

You may have heard the name Michelin with regard to automobile tires as well as delectable food. The origin of the prestigious Michelin Star for restaurant food began with the French Michelin Company founded in the late 1800s by brothers André Michelin and Édouard Michelin. The company was known for manufacturing tires at a time in history when automobiles were emerging as a great way to get around instead of by foot, bike, horse-drawn carriage, or train.

Wanting to encourage people to buy more cars, the brothers created a red-covered handbook called the *Michelin Guide* for motorists. The guide included tidbits on tire repair, car mechanics, maps, and hotels. Eventually the guides included information about restaurants and began to rate restaurant food with one to three stars for the overall quality, flavor consistency, and presentation.

Today chefs around the world often seek the prestige of earning and maintaining the Michelin Star (or two or three) as a benchmark for excellence. Michelin published its first American guide in 2005. The ratings are determined by anonymous inspectors who dine at restaurants.

The demanding elements of earning and keeping the star require a great deal of work.

Caroline started as a line cook at the Spotted Pig and after two years became a sous-chef under well-known British chef April Bloomfield. "I loved April's palate, and I loved every single dish," Caroline says. "We were going to the farmers market and getting fresh produce and working with the best of the best. It really formed who I am as a cook."

But the days were long and grueling. Caroline would go to work in the early afternoon and then stay until the early hours of the morning. "It was the hardest and most challenging job I've ever had. I definitely cried a lot at the beginning because I was so homesick." After two years at the Spotted Pig, Caroline felt burned out and was ready for change.

A good friend of hers worked at the Eckerton Hill Farm in Berks County, Pennsylvania, and would rave about being there. The farm grows hundreds of varieties of organic fruits and vegetables that are sold to New York City restaurants as well as the New York's Union Square Farmers Market.

The farm work sounded amazing, and Caroline was eager to get out of the city. She started to farm at Eckerton Hill on weekends, and then she eventually moved to Pennsylvania to work there full time.

Farming appealed to Caroline's desire to work hard and learn more about where food comes from. It was an important time in her life to regroup and be outside in nature. It was also a significant moment for her because she met her fiancé, Nelson Harvey, at Eckerton Hill. The two started dating and then moved east to Vermont to work at a large four-season vegetable farm called Pete's Greens.

After living and working in Vermont, Caroline and Nelson moved west to Colorado to continue working at various farms in small towns such as Paonia and Carbondale. Their longest stay was at the Fresh and Wyld Farmhouse Inn in Paonia where they farmed. Caroline also cooked food for the inn. Although she missed the East Coast, she definitely liked the Colorado sunshine and weather.

In 2014, Caroline and Nelson moved to Denver to build a life there. They got married in 2016 at Nelson's family's ranch in western Colorado.

Caroline started working at Acorn Restaurant in Denver and was eventually promoted to sous-chef under executive chef Amos Watts. But deep down she felt frustrated because she had bigger life dreams and wanted to do more. "I just felt uninspired, and I wasn't done learning. I definitely knew I wanted to open a restaurant at some point."

After two years at Acorn, the timing seemed right. In the fall of 2016, Caroline opened Annette in a family-oriented neighborhood of Aurora, Colorado, called Central Park. Figuring out a name was easy. She named her restaurant after her beloved great aunt, Annette, whom everyone called Netsie.

"Netsie was a big part of my life," Caroline says. "I grew up in a conservative household, and we didn't discuss a lot of things at our dinner table. But Netsie was kind of like the wild card. She loved talking about politics, and I saw that spark in her and was enamored with it. I really looked up to her because she was a strong, independent woman."

When it was time for Caroline to create the menu for Annette, she drew from cherished foods and flavors from her childhood in Texas, and she included homemade dishes and wood-fired fare. Most of her dishes are made from scratch, and her restaurant's tagline is "Scratch to Table."

She uses many fresh fruits and vegetables from local farmers. "Our menu changes so much," she says. "I like working with things that are in season."

At Annette, diners will find unique dishes such as sea island red peas and cauliflower, buckwheat and celery pasta, Wagyu beef grilled burgers with fries, and grilled beef tongue with beet relish. For dessert, Caroline features her mother's favorite pecan pie, and kolaches, a sweet or savory Czech pastry that Netsie loved, are often served for brunch.

In designing Annette, Caroline put her heart and soul into creating a cozy atmosphere for diners as if they were guests at a dinner party in her own home. Her restaurant has a small dining room with an open kitchen so diners can watch food being prepared. She also worked hard to build an exceptional team of chefs and servers. Her husband, Nelson; her sous-chef, Chelsey Maschhoff; her general manager, Daniel Seibel;

and her line cook, Jacob Taggs, have been at Annette from day one.

Soon after opening Annette, Caroline began to receive praise and distinguished awards. But in March 2020, everything changed with COVID-19. The restaurant she had worked so incredibly hard to bring to life was temporarily shut down. Caroline, Nelson, and the team were devastated. "It was a whirlwind," Caroline says. "The town of Aurora shut us down on a Saturday, and by Sunday we came up with a game plan." Their game plan consisted of burgers to go for about three to four months. But over time, takeout wasn't cutting it.

In the summer of 2020, Caroline and Nelson read about how restaurants in Amsterdam were serving diners in small greenhouses to follow social-distancing guidelines. This idea appealed to them. In August they purchased 12 small see-through greenhouses and one large yurt for bigger parties. Nelson put the word out on social media that volunteers were needed to help build the structures. The response was immediate, and about 25 volunteers showed up to help build the greenhouses.

Each greenhouse had a decorative table and chairs for two as well as power for lighting, music, fans, heaters, a handy service button, and a QR (Quick Response) code for ordering food. "I think we were the first restaurant in Colorado, if not the United States, that put up greenhouses," Caroline says. "COVID made me realize how strong we are, how resilient we are, but also how fragile we are. People ordering from us and supporting us was the biggest takeaway for me."

Today, Annette is back to business and stronger than ever from the challenges of surviving the very hard times of COVID-19. Yet through it all, Caroline has always stayed on track with her desire to do what she loves to do most—make delicious food and make people happy. It has given her life meaning and direction. "Learning to cook and feeding people has been a very healing thing for me."

Caroline's Favorites

Time of day: Morning. It's the time I get to work out, meditate, and have a few moments with my husband, Nelson.

Time of year: Fall. Summer is hot here in Denver, and fall is such a fresh breath of air for me. Getting to see the leaves change on an autumn hike is really indescribable.

Place on Earth: At the top of a mountain with Nelson.

Food to cook: Beer-can chicken on the grill or a grilled whole fish with some fresh vegetables. Cooking simple food in the backyard over a fire is my jam.

Food to eat: Any home-cooked meal that I don't have to cook. It's always such a treat to have someone else cook for you in their home.

Saying: "When the going gets weird, the weird turn pro." —Hunter S. Thompson.

Mentor: I'm not sure I have one. I've learned so much from so many different people.

Book: Any cookbook by American chef and food activist Alice Waters.

Follow Caroline Glover Online

Website: www.annettescratchtotable.com

Instagram: @caroglover8; @Annette_scratchtotable

Facebook: @annettescratchtotable

Cheetie Kumar:
Rock Star Chef

When Cheetie Kumar was eight-and-a-half years old, her family moved from India to the United States. She absolutely couldn't wait to get there. After combing through Sears catalogs and peering at fancy *New York Times* print ads of high-end cars and delicious-looking convenience foods, Cheetie was eager to be in her new home in America. She envisioned an immaculate world of Hoover vacuum cleaners and spotless air-conditioned abodes. "I imagined a cushy, very civilized, polite life."

But that's not exactly what happened.

Cheetie's family moved to a two-bedroom apartment on the 20th floor of a high-rise building in the Bronx, a borough of New York City. The sights and sounds of her new neighborhood were intense. "We lived across the street from a hospital," she says. "The ambulances were constant, and that sound really carries."

The nearby park was pretty, but Cheetie says it was a haven for unsavory folks and drug dealers. Even walking to school meant getting catcalls along the way. She was happy that her neighborhood was diverse with families from all over the world, but she felt isolated and caught between two cultures. Although she spoke English, Cheetie felt like she had two different accents—one she used at home with her family and another she used at school to fit in. On top of everything, making friends was rough. "There just weren't that many Indian people in our neighborhood at all. The whole thing was just awful and traumatizing."

But Cheetie was determined to be happy. High above the city in her apartment she found joy in two main activities—music and cooking. It was her happy escape that eventually morphed into an ongoing lifestyle and career.

Cheetie Kumar is the acclaimed chef of Garland Restaurant in Raleigh, North Carolina. She co-owns Garland with her husband, Paul Siler, in downtown Raleigh. The couple also co-owns the Kings and Neptune's Parlour music venues. In addition to her work as a chef, Cheetie plays guitar and sings in the popular rock band Birds of Avalon with Paul.

Cheetie grew up in Chandigarh, India, which is located in the Punjab region of the northern part of India, not far from the Himalaya mountains. "Chandigarh is a landlocked city, fairly small by Indian standards, but very populated," she says. "It has very modernist architecture interspersed with sort of the Indian landscape. Picture modern traffic circles with a couple of cows resting on them and wide boulevards shared by rickshaw drivers, three-wheel scooters, and an onion vendor pushing his cart."

As a young girl, she lived in a two-story bungalow with her older sister, younger brother, parents, and her paternal grandmother. Her mom and dad worked as research scientists in immunology at a local university. When her parents were not available to drive her to school, Cheetie and a few friends would ride in a rickshaw to get there.

The weather of Chandigarh could be extremely hot or cold, followed by the sweet-smelling rain of the monsoon season. "I wore a uniform to school and remember getting a prickly heat rash on my chest because it was just so hot," she says.

Cheetie loved playing outside and riding her bike up and down the streets of Chandigarh. The beeping of car horns was an ever-present hum in the background. Inside her home, the spice-laden smells coming from the kitchen were enticing. Cheetie spent hours in the kitchen with her mother and grandmother preparing food. "My mother was my big culinary influence, and she was a really excellent and meticulous cook who was constantly evolving and adventurous. If she had had a different kind of life, I think she would have been a chef. She was absolutely dedicated to making sure that we ate home-cooked meals every day."

Cheetie remembers some of her favorite dishes growing up. "Mom always had a pot of *dal makhani* on the stove. This is a stew-lentil dish that is typical of the Punjab region. She made an amazing *rajma* dish with kidney beans, and the most excellent parathas, which were stuffed flatbreads."

Cheetie ate tons of oranges, mangoes, pomegranates, and tangerines, and she was also very fond of sweets such as peanut or sesame brittle. But one of her all-time favorite savory foods that her mom made was the unusual-looking bitter melon.

What's Bitter Melon?

Bitter melon (*Momordica charantia*) is an oblong-shaped vegetable that has a waxy, thick green or yellow skin that can be warty and bumpy looking, or somewhat smooth. It grows hanging from a vine and is also known as bitter gourd, bitter apple, bitter squash, or balsam pear. Bitter melon is part of the gourd family and has similarities to cucumbers, chayote squash, or bell peppers, and is considered one of the most bitter foods on Earth. Bitter melon is native to Asia, Africa, and the Caribbean, and is often eaten throughout India, especially northern India. It is high in fiber and antioxidants, and some people believe the bitter melon has medicinal qualities such as being a digestive aid and helping regulate blood sugar levels in the body.

Bitter melon can be eaten raw or cooked, and it is often used in stir-fry recipes. Once the melon is cut in half, the interior has a colorful seedy pulp that can be scooped out. The vegetable can be then cut up in narrow sections and cooked with other ingredients such as garlic, mushrooms, eggs, and ground pork.

Cheetie's interest in music began in Chandigarh. "I liked to listen to music and sing, but only when I was alone. I learned all the Beatles harmonies. I was also in drama club and school plays."

Music then became an integral part of her life in the Bronx, and she says it was a great way to make friends. When she was older, Cheetie was into rock bands such as the Pretenders, the Cars, and Blondie. She also liked the punk rock band the Ramones. "I was obsessed with music. I would spend a good amount of my life listening to music, listening to and taping songs off the radio, being obsessed with bands, and talking about music to whoever was interested."

Eager to play an instrument, she picked up her sister's acoustic guitar and started to teach herself how to play basic chords. Soon she wanted to learn more. "I took this weird folk guitar class that was six weeks long that I hated at a community center in the Bronx. I didn't want to learn how to play, 'Down in the Valley,' I wanted to play rock songs."

When Cheetie was about 13, her brother gave her a Led Zeppelin music book and she learned a few chords of the song, "Stairway to Heaven." She eventually got her first guitar, which was a Fender Telecaster Deluxe 1972.

And when she wasn't listening to music or figuring out how to play guitar, she was busy in the kitchen getting dinner ready for her family. This was her primary chore while her parents were at work. In time she became more confident in the kitchen and began to enjoy the responsibilities her mom gave her. "I could actually start the rice instead of just soaking it. I could get the lentils to where they were ready for their final stage."

After graduating from high school, Cheetie headed to college at the University of Massachusetts in Amherst. Her major was psychology with a double minor in comparative literature and history. And once her homework was done, she quickly threw herself into her favorite subject—music.

As a sophomore, Cheetie became a DJ at a small radio station in the basement of her dorm. "I got the really late-night Sunday shift, which was great. I carried my records in a milk crate downstairs, and I learned to operate a really old audio board with knobs and faders."

She then got a job as a promotions director at WMUA 91.1 FM, the main radio station on campus. Suddenly Cheetie was promoting local Amherst bands and venues and giving away concert tickets. "It was back-end music business stuff, which was really fun for me."

She enjoyed the work so much it became the start of a career that took her to a whole new city. After leaving UMass, Cheetie moved to Raleigh, North Carolina, with a friend from the station. Cheetie instantly fell in love with the city. "I recognized the culture in North Carolina as one that was food centric with a long, rich, and sometimes painful history—much like that of my native Punjab."

It wasn't long before she landed a publicity internship at a local record company in Raleigh. She also found another job at a small company that managed bands and did everything from booking tours, to making sure records were on schedule, to booking studio time.

After living in Raleigh for about four years, Cheetie met Paul Siler, who would become her husband, her rock star companion, and her business partner. It was clear that Cheetie and Paul had many interests in common that unfolded over time.

One huge interest was performing onstage. In 1998 Cheetie and Paul started playing in a garage rock band called Cherry Valance. Paul played bass and Cheetie played guitar. At first, Cheetie stood off to one side of the stage and didn't use a microphone. "I liked being in the shadows."

But when Cheetie began writing and engineering songs in a local production studio, she started to find her own voice. "It was easier for me to sing in the studio because I could do it by myself. But then once the song was written with my voice on it, I had to do it live." And when she began to play guitar and sing on stage, she was a big hit.

On top of touring, performing, and releasing albums, the couple continued to stretch their wings and take on new creative adventures. In 1999, Paul helped open a music and bar venue in Raleigh called Kings that attracted local and national bands. It was an exciting time, and Cheetie was busy helping run Kings and manage the bar.

About six years later, Cheetie and Paul formed a popular new rock band called Birds of Avalon that is still active today.

Nonetheless, challenges arose. The building where Kings was located was torn down in 2007, so Cheetie and Paul needed to scout downtown Raleigh for a whole new space. They eventually found a large multilevel building on Martin Street and opened Neptune's Parlour, a basement cocktail bar with music, during the summer of 2010. That August they opened the new Kings music venue, and suddenly, music was booming and things were hopping again.

About four years later, one of Cheetie's biggest dreams came true. She had always wanted to open an eatery, and in 2014 she and Paul opened a restaurant on the main floor of the building on Martin Street. Cheetie named the eatery Garland. Although she had no formal culinary training, she confidently became the restaurant's main chef. "We had blind optimism and blind ambition," she says. "I think if you realized how hard it was going to be, you'd never do it. There was definitely an element of naivete in it."

The name of the restaurant had special meaning for Cheetie. Garlands are constructed with flowers and leaves and are worn or draped outside homes and temples in India. "Garlands are a whole made from many disparate parts. I really loved how that spoke to what our food was going to be because it wasn't like a singular focus. It was a lot of different flavors and concepts."

Cheetie draws from her childhood food favorites, world travel, and research to create seasonal menus that use local crops. "Our menu is an expression of North Carolina's seasons and ingredients expressed through the pantry of South, West, and East Asia, and not so much the Far East."

For example, a few items on the Garland menu have included Punjabi ratatouille pie, lamb kofta stuffed pepper, and North Carolina watermelon and peanut *chaat.* Cheetie loves that many of the North Carolina ingredients she uses are similar to foods found in northern India. "There's a tropical part of the summer in India we don't have in North Carolina. But here in Raleigh we have mustard greens and carrots and purple-top turnips in the winter. In summer we have okra and tomatoes and eggplants. That's literally identical to what we have in India."

Her new venture with Garland has been a success and has expanded her circle of friends and colleagues in a whole new way. Five years after opening the restaurant, Cheetie became involved with an innovative food project called Brown in the South.

Brown in the South

In 2018, chefs Meherwan Irani and Vishwesh Bhatt created a series of collaborative dinners featuring acclaimed chefs of Indian origin who have made the American South their home. They coined their concept, "Brown in the South," and Cheetie was one of the first chefs to be featured in the series. In addition to preparing and enjoying delicious food, BITS was designed to encourage conversation and discussion about what it means to live and work in the South for a person of Indian descent. Having a sense of belonging was key. The series also explores the parallels between Indian and Southern cuisine with a look at the many similar ingredients such as greens, black-eyed peas, okra, rice, and sweet potatoes that are grown in India and the South. Money earned from Brown in the South dinners benefits the Southern Foodways Alliance, which "documents, studies, and explores the diverse food cultures of the changing American South." The SFA is located at the Center for the Study of Southern Culture at the University of Mississippi. For more info go to www.browninthesouth.com.

It hasn't taken long for people to notice Cheetie's delicious and distinctive food. Over the years she has been nominated for a number of James Beard Awards including: Semifinalist, Best Chef, Southeast in 2017, 2018, 2019; and a finalist nominee for Best Chef, Southeast in 2020.

And then, when COVID-19 hit in 2020, Cheetie and Paul were forced to find creative ways to continue providing food at Garland. Kings and Neptune's were temporarily closed, and the Birds of Avalon band took a COVID-19 sabbatical. Cheetie was happy the band started rehearsing again in 2021.

Are there parallels to being a rock star and a chef? Cheetie says there definitely are. "I think both of them are really about understanding your own creative process and trying to figure out the best way to take an idea and express yourself through it in whatever way represents you. And you get to decide that. There are not many times in life where you can really decide how to portray yourself and how you're received or perceived. And that really opens up a whole psychological and sometimes emotional Pandora's box."

Cheetie added that playing an instrument onstage or cooking food for others is a collaborative process that involves teamwork. And, she says, it isn't about magic. "When you're playing guitar, you don't just magically become a great guitar player. You practice and a lot of humiliation happens. You mess up in front of people. It might be a big show and you totally screw up and everybody knows it's you. It's awful, but you learn," she says. "There's also muscle memory involved and coordinating an idea with your body is something that both realms have. When you're cooking, you're in a situation where it could be dangerous. You're working with heat and knives. The way your knife skills are can really affect the outcome of a dish just in the same way your chops as a guitar player can really affect the outcome of a song."

Muscle Memory

Chefs often talk about having muscle memory while working in a kitchen. Muscle memory is the result of the continuing practice and repetition of an activity so a person can remember a movement without having to think about it. It becomes a natural movement.

People working in a kitchen need to be able to work and move efficiently and safely around one another as well as around the stove, sink, counters, shelves, appliances, and tools. A chef's kitchen is often a confined space and one wrong move could mean trouble.

In addition to working in a kitchen, muscle memory is important for many activities such as dance, playing an instrument, typing, playing a sport, riding a bike, driving a car, and gymnastics, to name a few.

Cheetie's advice for someone wanting to become a chef? She feels that a person needs to be prepared to work really hard because there are no shortcuts and there are always new things to learn from mentors willing to share their knowledge. She says that being a chef requires a strong background with food as well as business and computer know-how. Even skills such as fixing a sink, cleaning a floor, or sharpening a knife can be crucial.

And, what does she think is most important? "Make sure you're always inspired and finding joy in food."

Cheetie's Favorites

Time of day: Sunset.

Time of year: Spring.

Place on Earth: A table full of food and friends.

Food to prepare: Anything in season.

Food to eat: I like to eat and I can't choose.

Song to sing: Anything in my range!

Saying: "All things must pass."

Movies: *The Godfather, Hiroshima Mon Amour, Chinatown, Caddyshack, Amadeus, 8½.*

Book: *Vegetarian Cooking for Everyone* by Deborah Madison.

Follow Cheetie Kumar Online

Website: Garland Restaurant, garlandraleigh.com; Birds of Avalon, birdsofavalon.com

Instagram: @cheetieku

Twitter: @cheetieku

Facebook: @garlandrestaurant

Tracy Obolsky: Pastry Chef and Surfer

During the last week of January 2016, a massive blizzard walloped New York City. Buried under more than 25 inches of snow, Manhattan was almost brought to a standstill.

Tracy Obolsky looked out her window and worried about getting to the high-end restaurant where she worked. On a clear day, her commute from the Rockaway Peninsula to Manhattan was already long and taxing. Right now it looked absolutely ominous. "The snowstorm was a doozy," Tracy says. "I told my boss the day before that I was concerned about not being able to get home if I came in."

Nonetheless, she was needed in the kitchen on that cold snowy day to make her signature pastries and desserts. As normal, Tracy got up at the crack of dawn to get ready for work. She put on her thickest coat, ski goggles, scarf, and gloves, and headed out to grab the A train subway. "As I was going over the bridge on the subway that goes over Jamaica Bay, you couldn't even see out the windows there was so much snow. An hour after I got to work, there were no more subway trains to get back to Rockaway."

Although Tracy considered walking all the way home that day, she wound up spending the night at a friend's house in Manhattan. Being trapped in the city was rough, but it proved to be a turning point for her life.

Tracy eventually quit her job at the restaurant in Manhattan and found work closer to her home on the peninsula. Not only was it near the Rockaway Beach where she loved to surf but also her commute to work would now be by foot, bike, or skateboard.

Even though visibility was bad during the New York City blizzard of 2016, the storm enabled Tracy to have a crystal-clear view of a whole new future.

Best thing of all? It was full of sweet surprises.

Tracy Obolsky is an accomplished pastry chef and the founder and owner of the Rockaway Beach Bakery in Far Rockaway, New York. She opened her popular surf-themed bakery in 2017.

Tracy was born in Paterson, New Jersey, and grew up in the nearby towns of Passaic and Clifton. Her home in Clifton was on a steep hill, and Tracy says it was super fun to sled on it when it snowed or race down it on any kind of device with wheels. She grew up with two younger brothers and had many close friends who lived on her tree-lined block. "We would walk everywhere together, and we built igloos on the front lawn. Now that I think about it," she smiles, "my neighborhood was really nice."

When Tracy was in middle school, hockey and snowboarding were "huge" in her life. She would snowboard at the Mountain Creek Resort in Vernon, New Jersey, which was about an hour's drive from Clifton. "It was always super icy there, and that's where I learned to snowboard. But if you can snowboard on ice, you can snowboard anywhere."

And even though she took her fair share of bad falls, Tracy still loved to snowboard the half-pipe, slide down handrails, and do jumps. "I was an obsessive snowboarder, and I grew up doing that with all the boys."

The sport led her to exciting new places and people. During spring breaks in high school and college she would head west to snowboard at the ski resorts of Vail and Steamboat Springs in Colorado. Years later she met her husband, Alex, at a ski shop in Manhattan where she was working at the time.

Food was an important part of Tracy's childhood home, and everyone always ate dinner together. There were festive holiday meals with platefuls of cookies brought over by her mom's two sisters. "My family was super into food, and my mom cooked every night," she says. "I ate everything growing up, and I was never a picky eater. You might say I was a weird eater in that I remember eating cold beets out of a can."

But as far as baking delicious cakes, pies, or cookies, Tracy's expertise as a pastry chef was inspired from her maternal grandmother, who was an excellent baker and made sought-after prune cakes and coffee cakes. "Grandma Helen passed away when I was like a year and a half, so I didn't really know her. But I have a lot of her recipes, which I still use."

Did Tracy hang out in the kitchen with her mom or dad and learn how to cook as a child? Not exactly. She was busy doing other things. "My dad was always taking me to hockey games or old car shows. I also grew up going to antique stores and estate sales, which I hated. I wanted to look at the new stuff like socks, hats, sunglasses, and pickles—not cut glass."

When it was time for college she wasn't sure what she wanted to study. "My family was like, 'You have to go to college.' But how do you know what you want to do when you're 17?"

There was one thing she knew she was good at. During her childhood, Tracy was skilled at drawing and painting, and she'd sometimes win magazine art contests. As a fan of the kids' books by Dr. Seuss and Shel Silverstein, Tracy had visions of illustrating a children's book one day. "I always did well in art, maybe not so well in the other subjects," she says. "Art was the only thing I could do."

In 2000, Tracy headed to the Pratt Institute in Brooklyn to study illustration. She had classes at both Pratt's Manhattan and Brooklyn campuses. For the first two years Tracy lived in the school dorms, and then she lived in various apartments in Brooklyn.

After being at Pratt for about a year, Tracy had the shock of her life. On September 11, 2001, she was sitting in an art class in Manhattan when two planes hit the World Trade Center towers. It was frightening, and she quickly rushed outside with other students to get out of the building. "We heard there had been a terrorist attack, and I didn't even know what that really meant. We saw all these businessmen running with briefcases, and we couldn't see down the street. It was just all smoke."

Tracy couldn't use her phone to call her parents or take the train anywhere. She wound up walking from a friend's apartment in Manhattan to Brooklyn to get away. "I was scared, and I just wanted to go home." She says she couldn't get home but was finally able to talk with her mom over the phone. She also couldn't go to school for a week and passed the time playing volleyball.

Tracy stuck with her studies at Pratt and three years later, at 22, she earned her bachelor of fine arts.

In 2006, Tracy married Alex, a boyfriend she met when she worked at a ski shop on 22nd Street in Manhattan. On a whim they decided to get married in Las Vegas. "Elvis married us and then he sang 'Viva Las Vegas,' after he pronounced us man and wife," she laughs.

Tracy and Alex moved into an apartment in Brooklyn. But her interest in art had waned, and she wasn't eager to find work in her field. Instead, she made money by bartending three nights a week for a few years. And with her free time during the day, Tracy started to cook more at home. She also began to watch TV cooking shows, which was an important turning point for her. "I was watching this *Ace of Cakes* show, and I'm like, I can totally do this because of my background in art. I love food. I love eating. This is what I should do!"

Tracy definitely wanted to do more with her life. She knew bartending wasn't going to last forever, and she wanted to excel at something. "I knew I wanted to be awesome at something, and I wanted to find a second career choice."

Next step? Tracy enrolled in an intensive half-year pastry program at the French Culinary Institute, now part of the Institute of Culinary Education, in artsy SoHo located in Lower Manhattan. Now 25 years old, her life had a new start, and she was bursting with energy. "I was really excited. It was like the first day of school for me, and my gosh, I got to do school all over again," she says. "I decided I was going to get the attendance award and never miss a day. I got a redo for all the mess-ups in my previous school life."

Duties of a Pastry Chef

Although pastry chefs create all sorts of attractive and scrumptious desserts and baked goods, it's not all sugar and spice. There are many important skill sets that are needed to succeed in this line of work. Being a team player matters because pastry chefs work with many other cooks who are often working in close quarters.

Pastry chefs typically work in restaurants, and the workload can be intense. The job often requires physical stamina as shifts can start early and last for many hours with constant standing on one's feet and moving around the kitchen.

Pastry chefs need to be able to work with recipes or create entire new ones. They need to be able to come up with a wide variety of pastries, breads, and desserts including ice creams, custards, and sorbets. Recipes for food items are either made from scratch or are used from a restaurant's existing one.

In addition to baking, pastry chefs are often responsible for scheduling, training, and supervising staff, as well as buying ingredients and managing cost control. At the end of a shift there are also pots, pans, tools, and counters to scrub down.

Tracy was thrilled with culinary school, and Alex was very supportive. But some of her family members were confused because she'd never shown a huge interest in cooking. "I mean, I burned the crap out of my hands making toast," Tracy admits. "But my family was also pumped because my grandma was a big baker, and they also loved baking."

Tracy took to culinary school with enthusiasm, writing down precise technique notes and attaching photos of foods to recipes. She learned many important baking skills, such as figuring out how to weigh and measure ingredients. She also learned how to make dough, decorate cakes, create ice creams and sorbets, make foamy meringues and fluffy souffles, create chocolate truffles, candies, jams, edible sculptures, and much more.

Her background in art turned out to be fortuitous. "A lot of the things that I learned in art school definitely translated really well and came in handy for sure. You always have to think about what the food looks like. So colors, composition. If you're doing a plated dessert, it needs to be appealing to the eye."

Tracy was a natural when it came to baking and says she only struggled for a short while with one complex dessert made with a cone-shaped tower of round cream puffs glazed with caramelized sugar. "I was having trouble with the croquembouche. It was frustrating because I kept burning my fingertips when I was dipping the pieces of pastry into hot caramel. But I eventually got it."

After graduating with a certificate of pastry arts from the French Culinary Institute in 2007, Tracy was eager to work in her field. It was already going really well. While at the FCI she landed a job in the pastry shop of the Borough Food and Drink restaurant on 22nd Street, right across from the ski shop where she once worked. "I was excited and eager to see how it was to work in the real world," she says. "The pastry chef ended up being my pastry mentor. I learned a lot, and the place was very ice cream driven and I started to really get into making ice cream."

Over the next few years Tracy learned a lot while working at a number of restaurants in New York City such as Madison and Vine, Five Napkin Burger, and General Greene. She continued to move up in her field.

Her first job as an executive pastry chef was in 2009 at the bustling, fine-dining Esca restaurant in the city, which specialized in Italian food and seafood. It was a very challenging job, and she stayed there for about four years making mouthwatering desserts such as vanilla mascarpone cheesecake with husk cherries, and affogato, which is an Italian coffee and espresso ice cream. Tracy liked to give this dessert an extra sparkle. "We always had affogato on the menu, but I would change it up. I made the ice cream, and then we put these chocolate Pop Rocks in it like candy. They would pop when you'd eat it. It was pretty cool."

Tracy was then hired as an executive pastry chef at the North End Grill in the city in 2013. By this time, she and Alex had moved from their place in Brooklyn to Far Rockaway where they were outside the city and closer to the ocean.

On the first day on the job at the North End Grill, Tracy met Meredith, a bartender, in the staff lunch line. They struck up a conversation, and Meredith, who was a surfer, encouraged

Tracy to surf with her at Rockaway Beach on the peninsula. Tracy decided to give it a try, and she and Meredith became fast friends.

In time Tracy became a skilled surfer. "Alex and I had taken a surf lesson on our first trip to Costa Rica and I loved it. It took me almost four years to learn to surf," she says. "It's hard and frustrating and exhausting. But once you start getting it, it's very exciting and awesome."

Tracy's smile grows wide when she talks about surfing with dolphins in the Rockaway Beach jetties. "Sometimes I feel like they're putting on a show for me. I've been by myself and I see them flipping. Sometimes they'll come really close and kind of play in between the surfers."

An avid sports buff, Tracy also loves to watch hockey. She had a unique chance to honor hockey at the North End Grill in 2014 when she created a dynamic one-of-a-kind ice cream treat.

Tracy's Red, White, and Blueshirts Ice Cream Sundae!

In June 2014 New York City was abuzz with excitement. The New York Rangers, nicknamed the Blueshirts, were playing against the Los Angeles Kings in the 2014 National Hockey League Stanley Cup Finals. Crowds poured into Madison Square Garden to watch the riveting game.

Although the Kings eventually defeated the Rangers, there were still some sweet moments to remember that summer. One moment included heading over to the North End Grill where Tracy worked. She had designed and created a special Red, White, and Blueshirts Sundae to honor the Rangers and the game of hockey, which she loves.

Her themed sundae was cleverly constructed of vanilla ice cream, berries, red velvet cake, and tiny blueshirt meringues on top. A special feature of the sundae was a thin chocolate cookie Tracy made to look like a miniature hockey stick. Fans loved it and the Rangers even stopped by the North End Grill to savor the flavor. The ice cream event was filmed and then posted on the Rangers' website.

"It was the best day of my life!" Tracy says.

Three years after starting at North End Grill, Tracy was hired at the Cookshop in Manhattan. Her commute from Far Rockaway to Manhattan wasn't easy, and when the 2016 blizzard hit the city, she was ready to say goodbye to the subway and her job.

Tracy was definitely ready to find work closer to home, and she teamed up with the owner of a pizza shop at a marina near the water. "It was basically a shack," she says.

But it was a new beginning. Tracy made pastries and coffee in the morning, and the pizza shop owner would make burgers and hot dogs in the afternoon. "It was so fun and the best summer ever. But it was getting very cold at the marina."

So Tracy found a new place in Far Rockaway to open her own bakery and named it the Rockaway Beach Bakery. An artist from Japan created her logo, which is an image of Tracy on a surfboard catching a wave and holding up a croissant.

Inside the bakery, Tracy painted her walls her favorite teal color and hand painted a large image of her logo on a main wall. Alex hung a surfboard that held speakers for music and built a surfboard planter with seashells that Tracy found at the beach.

Tracy bakes new goodies every day and often uses fruit with pies or pastries. One of her most popular items is a strawberry rhubarb pie. But there have been challenges. Her oven exploded one morning, and someone mysteriously ran off with the tip jar one day.

And then came COVID-19. Because Tracy already did a lot of takeout, she kept her bakery open during the pandemic. But it meant a lot more work of taking phone orders and constantly running bags of pastries from the kitchen to the front of the store and back. "You had to be very athletic. But it was either do that or—I mean I couldn't close the bakery. If I did there was no reopening."

Challenges aside, Tracy loves what she does. "I love the ability to be creative and make whatever I want. The possibilities are endless, and I get to do that based on the delicious things that are available at the time."

Tracy's Favorites

Time of day: Morning.

Time of year: Summer.

Place on Earth: Costa Rica.

Pastry to bake: Croissants.

Pastry to eat: Croissants.

Quote: "Dream as if you'll live forever. Live as if you'll die today." —James Dean.

Mentor: New York restaurateur Andy Menschel.

Song: "Say It Ain't So" by Weezer.

Movie: *Wayne's World*.

Follow Tracy Obolsky Online

Website: Rockaway Beach Bakery, www.rockawaybeach bakery.com

Instagram: @tracyobolsky; @rockawaybeachbakery

Twitter: @PastryChefTracy; @rockawaybbakery

Facebook: Tracy Obolsky

Part III
Food Activists

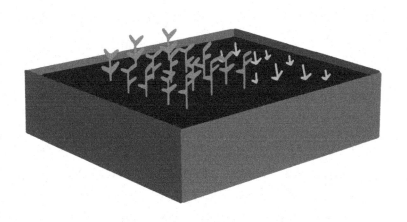

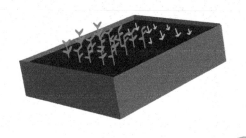

7

Dani Nierenberg: Mover, Shaker, Impact Maker

In 1996, Dani Nierenberg's first job out of college landed her 1,800 miles from home on a tropical island in the Caribbean. The hot humid weather, palm trees, food, and beaches appealed to her. But that's not why she was there. She was 22 years old and determined to make a difference in the world as a Peace Corps volunteer. For the next two-and-a-half years, Dani worked in the bustling city of San Francisco de Macorís of the Dominican Republic.

Stationed at her Peace Corps counterpart agency, which was the local Universidad Católica Nordestana (Northeast Catholic University), Dani worked out of a rooftop office. "It was a very open-air office," she laughs. Her focus was on environmental education, and it didn't take long for her to reach out to local extension workers, farmers, teachers, and students, and get right to work.

At the start, Dani helped build a tree nursery on the university campus that local farmers could use. She planted tropical fruit trees such as guava, kumquat, guanabana, and coffee. She also worked with inner-city elementary school teachers to create teaching materials and curriculum about the environment. Her students learned everything from how to compost and recycle to how to grow a seedling. During the summers, Dani also organized kids' camps based around environmental themes and activities.

But living in the Dominican Republic was a whole new world from her midwestern upbringing, and it was a big adjustment. After living for three months with a host family, Dani moved to a small housing complex she calls the "little compound." Her home was a bright blue brick bungalow with a tin roof she likened to a shack. "But I loved my little house. It was adorable." On many mornings chickens or coconuts would land with a thud on her tin roof and jolt her awake for the day.

The compound consisted of six bungalows and housed about a dozen people. Dani's home had a small living room with a kitchen in the front of the house and a back room that had her bed and a big plastic tub for bathing. Men and women of all ages shared one outdoor latrine and used one main outdoor water tap. "Whenever water would come, we'd all rush out to fill our buckets and containers for bathing."

Being a volunteer required stamina. "You're sick all the time and you're tired, and there weren't that many people I could talk with freely," Dani says. But she made good friends at the compound and felt that working as a Peace Corps volunteer in the Dominican Republic was exactly what she imagined it to be. "It was being with the community and making friends with people who were very different from the people I grew up with."

The Peace Corps is the brainchild of President John F. Kennedy, the 35th president of the United States, who founded the volunteer-based program in 1961. President Kennedy encouraged Americans to work in host countries around the world to promote democracy and peace and to learn about different cultures. Since 1961, nearly 240,000 volunteers have worked in 142 countries to date. For two-year time frames, volunteers serve abroad in a variety of positions from fighting hunger and disease to protecting the environment.

Dani admired the ingenuity and hard work of the Dominican farmers. "I would go visit farmers who were raising bees and trying to deal with a mite problem in a very natural way without pesticides. I once saw a farmer grab a bee without harming it and pick a tiny mite off it." She saw how farmers raised animals in sustainable ways and how they grew and protected the many crops and plants of their region. "I went into the Peace Corps very naive, like I was going to save the world. Yet I feel like the Peace Corps did the just the opposite. It saved me. I learned so much and figured out what I wanted to do in the world."

Dani Nierenberg is a food activist and the award-winning president of Food Tank, a worldwide think tank she cofounded in 2013. The mission of Food Tank is to build a global network of people and organizations to make sure the 7.9 billion people on our planet are nourished with safe and healthy food.

What's a Think Tank?

The term *think tank* sounds like a bunch of brainiacs swimming around an aquarium contemplating reality. Nope. Think tanks are typically privately funded nonprofits that work with individuals and organizations to shine spotlights on important issues such as hunger, health, poverty, climate change, technology, and housing. Think tanks have an important place in our world, and there are thousands of different ones across the globe, each with its own unique purpose. Think tanks bring awareness to world problems and advocate for solutions and change. Their typical goal is to conduct research to provide helpful information and ideas for individuals such as leaders, journalists, and decision makers. Ideally, change can occur with think tanks that help shape public policy via the creation of new laws.

Some people view think tanks as universities without students where evidence-based research is conducted, discussed, and brought forth. Some people, however, believe think tanks are negatively influenced by their donors. Think tanks have been around since the 1800s, and the earliest ones were often focused on military issues, such as defense.

Dani grew up in the small rural town of Defiance, Missouri—the town that legendary frontiersman Daniel Boone once called home. Nearly all of Dani's neighbors were farmers, and large corn and soy fields dotted the landscape. "Looking back, I didn't realize what an idyllic childhood I had until I became an adult. I had a big garden, and woods to play in, and a creek behind our home. In those days you could go out and play and come back before dark." Dani also had a pony named Sue that she rode in a paddock in her backyard. At one point she even raised pigeons.

Anything to do with food has always been a big part of Dani's life. "I was obsessed with food," she says. "I was the kid who was asking at breakfast what was for lunch and at lunch what was for dinner." Dani says that her mom would can anything that could fit in a jar and she was always canning and freezing foods. Today she calls her mom an original food waste warrior.

As Dani got older she developed into an ardent environmentalist, becoming a vegetarian when she was 13. She remembers going to a garage sale and finding a dog-eared copy of the groundbreaking book, *Diet for a Small Planet* by Frances Moore Lappé. Dani says the book blew her mind and changed her way of thinking about agriculture. "I blamed farmers for a lot of things like destroying the rainforest and producing cattle."

Diet for a Small Planet

Many books have been written about how farming and agricultural practices have impacted nutrition and the availability of food for Earth's inhabitants. Author and food activist Frances Moore Lappé was one of the first writers to tackle global food industry problems and specifically world hunger. Her 1971 bestseller, *Diet for a Small Planet*, described how the environmental impact of meat production and ineffective food policy added to food waste and scarcity. Frances advocated for vegetarianism in her book and provided simple guidelines for having a healthy diet with meat-free recipes. Frances was born in Oregon and started researching and writing *Diet for a Small Planet* when she was 26 years old and studying at Earlham College in Indiana. She has since written many books including *Hope's Edge: The Next Diet for a Small Planet*, which she wrote with her daughter Anna Lappé. Frances and Anna founded the Small Planet Institute in 2001 to provide solutions for our global food system.

During her later teen years, eating regular meals became hard for Dani and she developed an eating disorder. Over time, she recognized that her eating habits had become very unhealthy, and she was eventually able to turn them around. Dani wants others to know that "you can come out the other side of something that is difficult for you when you are young and be happy and healthy. You can turn it into something that you love."

Growing up in Defiance wasn't easy, and there were things Dani wanted to defy—like where she lived. She often felt like a big city girl living in the middle of nowhere, even though she admits she'd never been to a big city at the time. After graduating from high school, she was more than ready to get out of town, away from the barns, silos, cornfields, tractors, flannel shirts, and farmers. She needed change.

Dani decided to go to Monmouth College in Illinois and enrolled in an environmental studies program. When the program was ended, however, during her freshman year, she turned to her political science professor, Ira Smolensky, for advice. He became an important lifelong mentor and helped Dani create her own major. She eventually earned a bachelor of arts degree in environmental policy and government.

After graduating from Monmouth College and then working for years in the Dominican Republic, Dani was ready to head back to school. She began graduate studies for a master's degree in agriculture, food, and the environment at the Tufts University Friedman School of Nutrition Science and Policy in Boston, Massachusetts.

It was an exciting time in her life. While at Tufts, Dani found a dream job in 1999 when she interned for Worldwatch Institute, a nonprofit environmental research organization founded by Lester Brown and located in Washington, DC. She was truly happy about the internship. "If you asked me when I was a teenager where I'd want to work, it was the Worldwatch Institute." Two years later she was hired as a food and agriculture senior researcher at Worldwatch. Dani's responsibilities grew as she focused on global food needs and agricultural sustainability.

In 2009, Dani helped launch the Nourishing the Planet project at Worldwatch with Brian Halweil to study innovations in farming around the world. The project was funded in part by the Bill & Melinda Gates Foundation, and Dani had the opportunity to travel to Africa to investigate and blog about food problems and farming innovations there. She had already been to Kenya in her late twenties and was eager to return to Africa again.

Dani also faced personal challenges. She had recently lost her husband, Phil Saeli, who battled Hodgkin's lymphoma twice. "He was the person who taught me about resilience and love," she says.

Over the next year and a half, Dani traveled with her friend and Worldwatch colleague Bernard Pollack to 30 different sub-Saharan African countries to hear countless stories of what people were doing to produce food and alleviate hunger and poverty. "It became this incredible amalgam of different stories and different people," Dani says. "As the trip progressed, I went from trying to collect studies to finding more anecdotal information. I was really interested in people's quality of life and how things had transformed for them."

She says she learned about many different projects, "from the Alliance for a Green Revolution in Africa, which is very controversial, to small-scale fisher folk in Ghana who are drying fish to prevent food loss and food waste." She learned there were hundreds of exciting ways farmers were coming up with innovative techniques to grow crops. She also saw how farmers were having success with Indigenous farming practices that have worked for centuries.

To share these special stories, Dani blogged during her travels. One blog post talked about a unique farming idea in Nairobi: "In Kibera, Nairobi, the largest slum in Kenya, more than 1,000 women farmers are growing 'vertical' gardens in sacks full of dirt poked with holes, feeding their families and communities. These sacks have the potential to feed thousands of city dwellers while also providing a sustainable and easy-to-maintain source of income for urban farmers."

Women farmers really stood out for Dani as she journeyed from country to country. "Women feed many communities, and they're the nutritional gatekeepers. But people don't realize that women farmers don't often have the same access to resources as men, whether it's land or credit."

The culmination of Dani's and Bernard's work in Africa became part of the Worldwatch Institute's book, *2011 State of the World: Innovations that Nourish the Planet.* In the book's first chapter, "Charting a New Path to Eliminating Hunger," Dani writes about women in The Gambia, a small country in western Africa, who had formed a large women's oyster association. The women had dammed up part of the Gambia River for a year to allow the oysters to grow bigger. In the long run this helped bring in more money and food for their communities once the oysters were harvested.

Dani stretched her wings again in 2013 when she founded her own think tank, called the Food Tank, with Bernard Pollack. Today there are three full-time staff members, a number of interns, and a food justice fellow.

With Food Tank, Dani is determined to emphasize the good that people are doing around the world to combat hunger and poverty rather than focusing on all the ongoing problems of our world. "You have to highlight the solutions. You have to give people hope about what's working on the ground otherwise these problems just seem overwhelming— like climate change or deforestation."

But Dani says that people don't always understand the urgency of food issues. "There's a lot that can be done, but we have to do it now. We have to be the change we want to see in the world." To help promote change, Dani and her team have created an inspirational and informative Food Tank website, as well as a podcast and annual Food Tank Food Summits that bring thousands of food system leaders and participants together to share ideas and solutions.

When COVID-19 emerged, Dani saw firsthand how the virus exposed our fragile food systems. "What we have to do now is build a food system that can withstand a global shock like COVID-19, and any other global shock that comes down the line." Dani saw positive action during this global crisis when local farmers stepped up to provide food for their communities. "We've seen them pivot from selling food to restaurants to making sure food banks have enough food."

In 2020 Dani was the sixth recipient of the Julia Child Award for her work "as a global thought leader on a mission to build a more equitable food system and as a champion for underrepresented voices in the industry."

Julia Child—Lady of the Ladle

Julia Child was born in 1912 in Pasadena, California. She loved swimming, hiking, and playing basketball in her youth, and graduated from Smith College in 1934 with a degree in history. In 1942, during World War II, Julia moved to Washington, DC, to help with the war effort. "At the close of 1942, Child took up the position of junior research assistant with the Secret Intelligence Branch of the Office of Strategic Services (OSS), a forerunner to the CIA."

Julia married OSS employee Paul Child after the war. In 1948 they moved to Paris where Julia studied at Le Cordon Bleu cooking school. Julia and Paul moved to Cambridge, Massachusetts, in 1961, and this was the same year her groundbreaking book, *Mastering the Art of French Cooking* (co-written with Simone Beck and Louisette Bertholle) was published. After an author interview at the WGBH public television station in Boston, Julia was asked to host the award-winning *The French Chef* cooking show, which lasted from 1963 to 1973.

Julia Child donated her kitchen to the National Museum of American History in Washington, DC, in 2001. In 2015 the Julia Child Foundation created the Julia Child Award to honor individuals who have positively impacted American cuisine.

Julia Child has been a role model for Dani since she was young. One of her best memories was watching the Julia Child cooking show with her dad and then making some of Julia's dishes for her parents. "My life started out with admiring Julia Child. She was a woman on TV at a time when there weren't that many. She was her own person."

Since Dani's early years of living in a small farming town in the Midwest to today, she has traveled the globe and made great strides in helping promote a more sustainable food system for our world. "For a food system to be sustainable, it has to be economically, environmentally, and socially just," she says. "It has to make sure farmers are paid for what they're producing and that there's a system that's fair. Food systems need to provide safe, healthy food for people."

Dani's Favorites

Time of day: Evening. I like watching the sun go down on the balcony where my husband, Dr. William Burke, and I built a garden.

Time of year: Summer! I'm from the Midwest and was a Peace Corps volunteer in the Caribbean. I'm the only person I know who loves heat and humidity!

Food: I love mushrooms—almost every kind I've tried from porcinis and shiitakes to hen-of-the-woods. They're versatile and have a meaty, earthy quality that I love.

Song: "Into My Arms" by Nick Cave.

Mentor: Ira Smolensky. He was my political science professor and advisor at Monmouth College in Illinois when I was an undergrad.

Movie: *Food, Inc.*

Books: *Silent Spring* by Rachel Carson, *Diet for a Small Planet* by France Moore Lappé.

Follow Dani Nierenberg Online

Website: foodtank.com

Instagram: @foodtank

Twitter: @foodtank; @DaniNierenberg

YouTube: www.youtube.com/user/daniellenierenberg

8

Haleh Zandi: Kale Not Jail

After graduating with a master's degree in cultural anthropology, Haleh Zandi was eager to do good in the world and make positive change. To lend a helping hand, she began volunteering at San Quentin State Prison, which is a correctional facility for men on San Francisco Bay in California.

At San Quentin, Haleh volunteered with the Insight Garden Program at the prison's on-site native plant and flower garden. Over the years she's worked with hundreds of incarcerated men to help them learn about gardening and landscape design.

Although Haleh loved being involved with the program, working at the prison wasn't easy. "I had to go through a criminal background check, and then I was trained as a volunteer," she says. "I struggled with my decision to cooperate with a system that has a history of human rights abuses, but I wanted to bring this gardening education to people who didn't have access to it."

Every week at San Quentin, she would go through security and then begin class. "We would first sit in a circle with the men and do an opening meditation. Then we would do a check-in and get everyone's voice in the room to see how people were feeling."

After that, it was time to work in the garden. "That was the best part," Haleh says. The group planted and took care of a wide variety of flowers and vegetables that were then donated to the families of the men who had been in the program. Everyone would then return to the circle to cool off, reflect on the day's work, and participate in a two-hour class. The class covered topics such as the industrial food system, climate change, vocational gardening, and social justice movements.

"The men were very polite, and they would really appreciate having us come in," she says. But it was an emotional roller coaster for her at times. San Quentin was located in a beautiful area of San Francisco that overlooked the Golden Gate Bridge and nearby bay. Haleh found it hard to head out of the facility knowing the men she worked with could not. "I had the freedom to leave, but having the men have to stay there would be really, really tough. I would cry."

Haleh volunteered at San Quentin for nine years. From the start, she knew that some of the men would eventually leave the prison and need to find work. This was part of the inspiration behind developing her nonprofit organization, Planting Justice.

Haleh Zandi is a cofounder and strategic advisor at Planting Justice, a grassroots organization in California designed to grow healthy food, jobs, and community. Haleh began Planting Justice in 2008 with her partner, Gavin Raders. She is Iranian American and a land- and food-based activist who has spent a great deal of her life working to bring justice to issues she's passionate about, such as food equality for all, peace, and protection of Earth's natural resources.

Haleh was born in the small town of Fountain Valley, California, located in Orange County just minutes away from popular Southern California beaches. At a young age, she would take the bus to Newport Beach, where she loved to swim in the ocean and bodyboard. She was constantly on the go and would skate and bike everywhere. "I grew up in Orange County as it transitioned from orange fields and strawberry fields into suburban neighborhoods with a lot of corporations setting up shop."

Her parents separated when she and her older brother, Bijan, were young. "My father's from Iran, and my mom was born and raised in California," she says. "Her family is Norwegian."

Her dad moved to Long Beach after the separation, and Haleh also lived in that nearby coastal town some of the time.

Haleh says she was fortunate to attend good public schools while growing up, and she liked how culturally diverse her community was. "That was impactful for me, but it was also a very politically conservative area, and that was hard for me."

Her mom worked full time, so Haleh was responsible for herself most afternoons. "I spent a lot of time at my best friend Cindy's house," she says. "They are Vietnamese, and I got exposed to different family practices, different food, and a different religion. I also had another good friend named Alexis, who is Greek."

Haleh was on a swim team when she was younger, but her favorite sport was soccer, which she played from sixth to twelfth grade on a varsity and club team.

Before the separation, her mom prepared Persian food every day for the family. "I grew up on Persian food," Haleh says. She ate a lot of stews prepared with vegetables, beans, and herbs, as well as chicken, lamb, or beef kabobs. "We ate everything with rice, yogurt, and a flatbread called naan. And we always had a fresh plate of greens on the table called *sabzi*."

But, in time, her eating habits changed. "Because I lived in a single-parent household, I ate a lot of fast food every day for lunch and dinner. I was raised on fast food." She decided at that point that when she had children one day, she wanted them to eat better.

With a strong desire to learn more about world cultures and social justice movements, Haleh earned her bachelor of arts in cultural anthropology from the University of California, Santa

Cruz, in 2006. She then earned her master's degree in the same major from the California Institute of Integral Studies in San Francisco in 2009.

During this time, Haleh also worked at Peace Action West in Berkeley, California, and she volunteered at the Women of Color Resource Center in Oakland, California.

In 2005 she met her partner, Gavin Raders, in an archaeology training course at a community college in Santa Cruz. Although both of them chose not to pursue a career in archaeology, they did decide to pursue a relationship, start a nonprofit, and begin a family together.

Haleh and Gavin were like-minded, and they both worked as antiwar canvassers and fundraisers at Peace Action West. A great deal of their work throughout 2007 was approaching people's front doors. "We knocked on thousands of doors in the Bay Area as well as in Denver and Boulder, Colorado," Haleh says. "We encouraged people to write letters to Congress to end the war in Iraq, prevent war in Iran, and stop the proliferation of nuclear weapons."

As they traveled door-to-door, the young couple started to notice things they didn't like. Haleh realized how underutilized neighborhood landscapes were. "Too many homes were wasting water on lawns during an epic drought." Plus, she thought that more food should be grown in yards instead. She wondered how things could improve.

She and Gavin brainstormed ideas about creating a nonprofit that was solutions based and focused on food production while keeping the overuse of fossil fuels at bay. In addition, she says they wanted to counteract inequalities in the agriculture and food industry where many farm and restaurant workers experienced labor inequalities.

Their answer to the problem? They cofounded an organization called Planting Justice that would focus on four specific programs: education, a sliding-scale landscape service, urban farm and training centers, and grassroots fundraising. One year later they applied for and got their federal 501(c) business status, which meant they could operate as a nonprofit organization.

Money was tight the first few years, but their ingenuity flourished. Both Haleh and Gavin volunteered their time with Planting Justice, applied for food stamps and Medi-Cal (California's Medicaid health care program), and rented tools from the local tool-lending library. Haleh's dad loaned them $6,000 to buy their first truck so they could transport recycled redwood from torn-down fences that could be reused to build raised vegetable beds.

What's a Raised Garden Bed?

Vegetables, flowers, and herbs can definitely be planted directly in the soil of the earth. But many gardeners like to use raised beds that are constructed above the ground. This type of above-earth garden has a number of advantages. First, the gardener has control over selecting the type of nutrient-rich soil with compost where their plants will grow. Having a higher place to garden can make planting, growing, watering, weeding, and harvesting more accessible to reach. Watering plants and water drainage can be easier with a raised bed. And raised beds are often an efficient way to grow plants in backyards as well as in schoolyards, churchyards, or prison yards. Sometimes raised garden beds are used on rooftops or patios where space is limited.

There are many different ways to construct a raised bed, and rot-resistant woods such as cedar and redwood often work well and help plants retain water. Wood can be constructed in a square or rectangular formation and can be about one foot high to waist high (or higher). Some gardeners have also used metal or plastic boxes for their raised beds.

Gardeners need to think about placement of raised beds for adequate sunlight. And having an efficient watering system, such as drip irrigation, can be a plus.

They found their first clients through free ads with Craigslist and used their door-to-door canvassing skills to fundraise. "I canvassed a whole neighborhood near Lake Merritt in Oakland and raised $3,000 that first summer," Haleh says.

Slowly Haleh and Gavin began to make progress by building raised vegetable gardens in schools, places of worship, community gardens, and apartment complexes. They were excited when the Mandela MarketPlace group in West Oakland invited them to teach gardening skills at a local middle school that worked with the West Oakland Youth Standing Empowered (WYSE) program. The WYSE program was designed to help young people transform the health and well-being of their communities. "Together we built four raised beds on their campus and grew a tremendous amount of greens that we cooked in the classroom," she says. "Students were also taking the greens home to their families."

During this time, Haleh and Gavin were also volunteering at San Quentin State Prison with the Insight Garden Program. They spent five years convincing different wardens to allow the program to build a vegetable garden in the prison yard of the medium-security unit. "As soon as we were working with the men there, it was very clear that what they needed when they returned home was a job," she says. "I really tried to reflect on my privilege as a heteronormative woman, as a light-skinned person—the privilege that I have around police brutality, around having access to educational privilege. I really wanted to use all those privileges to help empower folks who didn't have the same access."

Beginning in 2010, Planting Justice began to hire formerly incarcerated men as part of their landscaping team. Their company's tagline became Kale Not Jail. "We continue to hire folks who are systems-impacted," Haleh says. "Not only are they getting immediate income—it's a living wage beginning at $19 per hour. We recognize that work within the agricultural field should be valued and that people deserve to get paid fairly."

They also work at Maple Street Correctional Center in Redwood City, California. "We have a garden there with about 80 plants growing in the ground there," she says.

Over the following years, Planting Justice began to grow and expand on more land. In 2014, Haleh and Gavin leased four acres of farmland from a cooperative called Wild and Radish in the small town of El Sobrante, located about 15 miles north of Oakland. "We've planted more than 2,000 varieties of fruit and nut trees, berry bushes, herbs, and other beneficial plants and flowers there," she says.

As Haleh worked as a nonprofit director and gardener, her roots in activism continued to grow. In 2016, Haleh, Gavin, their two young daughters, her mother, and a caravan of 30 other volunteers traveled to the Standing Rock Indian Reservation in North Dakota to protest the building of the Dakota Access Pipeline. Haleh and Gavin wanted their daughters to learn about this Indigenous-led movement to protect the region's land and water supply.

At the protest Haleh spoke with Native American elders who encouraged her to support the Indigenous people where they lived back home in California. When Haleh and Gavin returned to the Oakland area, they met Indigenous land-activist Corrina Gould, who was born and raised in Oakland. Corrina is Lisjan Ohlone and the tribal spokesperson for the

Confederated Villages of Lisjan Ohlone. She is a cofounder of the Sogorea Te' Land Trust, which is an urban, Native, and women-led land trust created in 2012 to protect Indigenous land in the San Francisco Bay area. Corrina cofounded the Sogorea Te' Land Trust with Johnella LaRose, a Shoshone Bannock and Carrizo grassroots organizer.

Meeting Corrina Gould proved to be an inspiring connection. In 2015, Haleh and Gavin were approached by the owners of the Rolling River Nursery, located in Northern California. The nursery grew hundreds of certified organic edible tree crops, and they had a thriving online sales website.

The Rolling River Nursery owners wanted to sell their business to a socially conscious organization and approached Planting Justice. The Planting Justice team was excited about investing in the nursery and got a community development loan to be able to purchase the business. Haleh was especially interested in acquiring a nursery with so many trees. "I feel a tremendous responsibility to plant a lot of trees. I want to make up for all the trees my Norwegian ancestors cut when they were coming from the Pacific Northwest down to California."

Planting Justice used the rest of their loan to purchase two acres of undeveloped land in East Oakland. In 2016 her team at Planting Justice rented 11 semitrailer trucks to transport more than 30,000 plants from the Rolling River Nursery collection. One of the favorite trees Haleh grows at their nursery today is the pomegranate. "We have more than 60 varieties of pomegranates in our nursery collection."

In 2017, Haleh and Gavin decided to propose that Planting Justice "rematriate" (return) the land back to the Ohlone people by agreeing to transfer the title of the land where Planting Justice operates its nursery to the Sogorea Te' Land Trust.

The Succulent Pomegranate

The pomegranate is a unique fruit that originated in Iran and the Himalaya region of northern India. The fruit is widely grown throughout South Asia and western states in the United States. Pomegranates were introduced to California by Spanish settlers in the mid-1700s.

Many pomegranates that are sold in grocery stores have a round red outer layer and are often found in the tropical fruit section. The fruit also comes in green, yellow, orange, purple, or pink varieties.

Pomegranates grow on bushy shrublike trees that have many trunks and red-orange flowers. The outer layer of the fruit is leathery and somewhat hard to cut into. But once inside the pomegranate there are hundreds of shiny fluid-filled edible seeds called arils. The arils are known to have antioxidants such as vitamins C and K. They are also high in fiber and have a sweet yet tart flavor. Pomegranates can be eaten directly, used as a garnish, or mashed to create products such as juice drinks, smoothies, syrup, and wine.

Over the past 10 years Planting Justice has built more than 550 gardens. But there are challenges. "Getting access to land long term is the biggest challenge," Haleh says. "And fundraising."

Nonetheless, she knows the deep rewards of the work she does. "Working in the garden is so healing. It's the most healing thing I've done besides having children," she says. "Working in a community builds deep relationships with people, and it's important for people to rebuild relationships with the earth. When you work in a garden, you learn that you can't control the garden. You need to learn to work with the cycles of nature. The most healing part is how you learn to be in a new relationship with Mother Earth—and how much she takes care of us."

Haleh's Favorites

Time of day: Sunrise. It's a time for quiet solitude when I stretch my body and practice meditation.

Time of year: Summer. This is when I enjoy berries, stone fruits, and melons.

Place on Earth: Standing Rock, North Dakota, for the way the Sioux Dakota and Lakota people inspired such an incredible movement against the fossil fuel industry. Plus, I was there with three generations of women in my family.

Food to eat: *Kookoo* sabzi, a Persian dish made with eggs and herbs which can be enjoyed for breakfast, lunch, or a late-night snack.

Food to grow: Pomegranates. The Planting Justice Nursery cultivates over 60 certified organic varieties of pomegranates, including a variety called Azadi which means "freedom," like my daughter's name, Azadeh.

Song: "Oh Sky" by Naima Shalhoub featuring Tarik "Excentrik" Kazaleh.

Saying: "Compost the Empire."

Mentor: Corrina Gould, cofounder of Sogorea Te' Land Trust and spokesperson for the Confederated Villages of Lisjan Ohlone.

Movie: *The Hunger Games* (Part 1).

Book: *The Clan of the Cave Bear* by Jean M. Auel. "I named our second daughter after the main character, Ayla."

Follow Haleh Zandi Online

Website: plantingjustice.org

Instagram: @planting.justice

Twitter: @plantingjustice

Facebook: @plantingjustice

Sheila Lucero:
Seafood Chef/Activist

In 2017 Executive Chef Sheila Lucero went from landlocked Denver, Colorado, to Washington, DC, to meet with members of Congress and policy makers on Capitol Hill. Sheila was part of Monterey Bay Aquarium's Blue Ribbon Task Force, head-quartered in Monterey, California. Her mission? To shed light on huge topics such as overfishing and to defend sustainable fisheries in the United States.

"The Blue Ribbon Task Force is a group of chefs across the country, and there's nearly 70 of us who work with the Monterey Bay Aquarium," Sheila says. "The aquarium brings us in for conferences and high-level education on the state of our oceans, our fisheries, and their Seafood Watch program. This has always been my guiding light for menu development."

It took courage to speak out in DC, and Sheila truly wanted to make a difference. "The whole thing was kind of surreal. I never really took politics super serious, but it was an honor to be there and meet so many passionate people who do care about our food systems. I saw and heard firsthand the power of our voices."

Wearing a crisp white chef's jacket, Sheila met with senators and representatives to present vital information about the health and sustainability of our oceans. Accompanying her were chefs Susan Feniger (of Border Grill restaurants in California) and Steve Phelps (of Indigenous Restaurant in Florida), as well as scientists and policy makers from the Monterey Bay Aquarium.

The trip to DC had a critical focus that involved standing up for key conservation objectives in the Magnuson-Stevens Fishery Conservation and Management Act (MSA), which was now up for review. Sheila explained that fundamental aspects of the MSA could be impacted and threatened by a newly proposed bill, H.R. 200, Strengthening Fishing Communities and Increasing Flexibility in Fisheries Management Act.

Along with scientists, policy makers, and hundreds of other concerned chefs, Sheila wasn't about to let this happen. She worked for months preparing for her many meetings with members of Congress from all across America. "I was proud to be representing a restaurant from an inland state that cares about our coasts and fisheries. The congressmen were shocked and attentive to what I had to say. We also had a lot of cool discussions about food and our food systems."

Sheila Lucero is the executive chef of Jax Fish House & Oyster Bar in Denver, Colorado. In addition, she oversees four other Jax Fish Houses in Colorado (Boulder, Fort Collins, Glendale, and Colorado Springs) as well as a Jax Fish House in Kansas City, Missouri. Sheila has been actively involved with a number of seafood programs including: Monterey Bay Aquarium's Seafood Watch program, the Blue Ocean Institute, Fish Choice, and the James Beard Foundation's Smart Catch and Bootcamps for Change programs.

The Magnuson-Stevens Fishery Conservation and Management Act

The oceans and waterways on Earth provide a significant food source as well as work and recreation opportunities for many people. Deciding how these waters are fished and managed matters on ecological and economical terms.

The Magnuson-Stevens Fishery Conservation and Management Act (MSA) was first passed by Congress in 1976 to regulate international fishing off the coastlines of the United States. It's "the primary law that governs marine fisheries management in US federal waters." The law was named after former US senators Warren

Magnuson, Democrat from Washington State, and Ted Stevens, Republican from Alaska.

Before 1976, international fishing boats could fish as close as 12 nautical miles from US shores. The MSA established new rules so that international fishing boats were to fish beyond 200 nautical miles from US shores. This ruling helped create more fishing opportunities for US fishers.

In addition, the MSA established eight regional fishery councils in the New England, mid-Atlantic, South Atlantic, Caribbean, Gulf of Mexico, Pacific, West Pacific, and North Pacific regions to enable locally driven fisheries management in the United States.

Years later, Congress amended the MSA two times.

In 1996, the Sustainable Fisheries Act was passed to prevent overfishing, to rebuild and to replenish overfished fisheries, to set national standards for fishery management and fishing safety and bycatch, and to protect fish habitat in fisheries management.

In 2006, the MSA Reauthorization Act was passed to require limits on what could be caught, to strengthen the role of science in fishing, and to strengthen international cooperation in fishing.

The MSA will continue to be scrutinized and updated for decades to come to find sustainable ways to manage US fisheries.

For more information, go to www.fisheries.noaa.gov /topic/laws-policies.

Sheila was born in Golden, Colorado, and grew up surrounded by the Rocky Mountains, open space, mountain streams, and beautiful wildlife. She grew up with a younger sister and brother, and her days were filled with going to school and an abundance of outdoor adventures.

"We had a great neighborhood where you could ride your bike and play in the street," she says. "We would play all kinds of games like tag, kick the can, hide and go seek, and capture the flag with our neighbors. I was definitely a tomboy and wanted to play football and ride a dirt bike like the boys."

When Sheila was about five or six years old, she began playing soccer, which she continued to play throughout her school years and college.

When she wasn't outside playing sports, Sheila was drawn to the kitchen where she developed a love for cooking from her dad. "He really enjoyed cooking for our family and still does. He loved to make things like enchiladas, and he was all about being patient with the process from start to finish. And I got to be a part of that."

Her dad is also a fan of green chilies. Every fall he drives to Pueblo, Colorado, to buy a variety of colorful spicy peppers, which he freezes and then uses throughout the year for his Mexican dishes. "Of course, it's all delicious," Sheila says. "It never really clicked as a kid that I wanted to be a chef. I just enjoyed being around him and cooking and eating. It wasn't until later in life that I realized there was definitely an influence there."

When it was time for college, Sheila enrolled as a biology major at Florida International University (FIU) in Miami in 1993, where she had a full scholarship to play Division I soccer. She left Colorado in August for FIU's preseason soccer program and was suddenly training and playing the game in a whole new environment of scorching hot and humid Miami weather. "It was a shock to my body, but I wanted to play soccer, so I dove deep into that and I loved my teammates and lifelong friends were made."

Sheila admits that soccer was grueling with a lot of travel, and it was hard to find a balance in her life. "I was not a great student then, and it wasn't a good fit. I didn't love Miami."

After about two years she left FIU and returned to Colorado, which didn't make her parents happy. Stymied and unsure of what to do with her life, she quickly headed to the mountain town of Breckenridge where she says she became a ski bum. "I worked at Breckenridge on the mountain teaching little kids how to ski and working lifts. I got so many days on the mountain, and it was exactly what I think I needed. I knew it wasn't going to be forever."

In time Sheila moved to Denver and started working in a bakery that had just opened. This proved to be a sweet, decisive moment in her life, and Sheila learned a great deal from the woman who owned and operated the Café Galileo bakery. "She was smart, classically trained, and went to culinary school. I connected with that whole scene and being in the kitchen and working with other people."

But Sheila still wasn't sure what to do with her life. Going to culinary school and getting a more formal training in the culinary arts seemed like an excellent idea. Unfortunately, her parents weren't gung ho about her new plan right off the bat and wondered if she was sure about her decision. They even reminded her she was just snowboarding.

After a long, drawn-out conversation with her mom and dad, Sheila convinced them that culinary school was exactly the right direction for her. In 1996, she enrolled in the School of Culinary Arts at the Colorado Institute of Art in Denver.

Suddenly her life started to sizzle! "I jumped in and fully immersed myself," she says. "I was one of the best students, and everything clicked for me. I was able to work and go to school and use that knowledge in real time. It just all came together, and I loved every minute of it."

To help pay tuition she was a line cook at the large Canyon Café southwest-style restaurant in Denver. "Holy cow, I learned a lot there. But it was one of those restaurants that had continual turnover, and you never really knew who was going to show up for work. Being young I was naive to some of the realities of this industry."

Sheila also got practical hands-on experience at her culinary school's restaurant. "The last two semesters you worked in a restaurant. You spent one semester in the front of the house and one semester in the back of the house. We would create menus and run a restaurant. We also had a lot of fun special events with different themes so we learned how to plan and organize. That was really cool."

In 1998 Sheila earned an associate's degree in culinary arts from her school and was soon hired as a line cook at a newly opened seafood restaurant in Denver called Jax Fish House & Oyster Bar owned by forward-thinking Colorado chef, Dave Query.

She was 24 years old and excited to begin work at Jax because she immediately noticed that the owner and staff were foodies and constantly talking about food. This felt like the right place for her. And preparing seafood was an exciting new venture. "I didn't eat a lot of seafood growing up in Colorado. So I was like, this is a good opportunity for me to learn something I don't know anything about."

And learn she did. Over the next 10 years Sheila went from line cook, to sous-chef, to executive chef at Jax in 2009. She was suddenly up to her starched sleeves in foods such as oysters, calamari, mussels, shrimp, crabs, and halibut. "I was so excited to pull on the back door and get there every day and talk about food and just be a part of it and learn. And still to this day I talk about that environment—that it's something we strive for in our restaurants culturally all the time. That's what we want to create. We want people to be excited to come to work."

Working with seafood is a unique aspect of the culinary arts. It has inherent challenges related to where fish comes from, how it's transported to a kitchen, how it's prepared, and if it's sustainably sourced. Sheila says that she pays attention to the seasons of fish, talks to vendors, watches the weather, and makes conscientious choices when sourcing seafood. "Guests probably don't see the homework and mindfulness behind the scenes. But they want to know where their food comes from."

In 2013 Sheila became a member of the Monterey Bay Aquarium's Blue Ribbon Task Force. In addition, the five Jax Fish House restaurants in Colorado were the first to be certified by the MBA Seafood Watch program in 2013. The sixth Jax restaurant in Missouri was certified in 2014. This certification means that the fish items on their menus are in the Best Choice category that indicates the fish population is well managed and caught or farmed responsibly in a fishery.

Monterey Bay Aquarium Seafood Watch Program

If you eat seafood, do you ever wonder how far that fish needed to travel to get to your table, or if it's in danger of being overfished or caught in a harmful way?

Launched in 1999, the Monterey Bay Aquarium Seafood Watch program helps consumers, seafood producers, and chefs obtain science-based information about sustainable seafood around the world. The Seafood Watch program offers a variety of consumer guides that list seafood in easy-to-read categories of: Best Choices, Good Alternatives, and Avoid.

Check out www.seafoodwatch.org/recommendations /download-consumer-guides.

After her trip to DC in 2017, Sheila's activism continued. About one year later she and a number of chefs traveled to Portland, Oregon, to participate in an exciting think tank. Together they wrote a letter to Congress called the Portland Pact, which was signed by nearly 200 chefs. The letter addressed key issues about keeping the MSA intact and maintaining sustainable practices for fishery management in the United States and throughout the world. They also launched a campaign called #Chefsforfish.

In 2018, Sheila returned to Capitol Hill to present the Portland Pact to Congress.

The Portland Pact Letter

"As chefs, we are passionate about serving the best food possible to our customers. This means using delicious ingredients produced without harming the planet. We strive to offer only environmentally sustainable food and to incorporate this principle into our sourcing practices whenever possible. Many of us have built our brands and reputations around this commitment.

"It is our business to ensure that US policies and regulations support and improve the domestic food systems and products we rely on in our kitchens and restaurants. When it comes to our seafood dishes, we must have a consistent supply of sustainably-caught fish—now and in the future.

"The Magnuson-Stevens Fishery Conservation and Management Act (MSA) is the primary law governing fishing in US waters. It has become a model for fisheries management around the world, successfully rebuilding fish populations and bringing overfishing to near all-time lows. The success of this policy to date has enabled us to offer a wider variety of domestic seafood that meets the environmental standards of our businesses.

"To maintain this progress, we must preserve the strong conservation measures of the MSA that prioritize the long-term health of US fish stocks over short-term economic gains, such as:

- Requiring management decisions be science-based;
- Avoiding overfishing with catch limits and tools that hold everyone accountable for the fish that they remove from the ocean; and
- Ensuring the timely recovery of depleted fish stocks.

"To keep our businesses and our oceans healthy, we support sustainably managed US fisheries and are committed to promoting the continued success of the MSA."

Since that time, Sheila has continued to be a strong advocate for sourcing seafood in sustainable and responsible ways, even during challenging times such as COVID-19. "Things are so crazy with COVID, and it's very different now. Ideally, we want fresh fish, so that's our goal. There are a lot of ways—with refrigeration and ice, and trucks and planes—to get food to Colorado. We're really mindful of where we're getting our food and how we're treating our oceans," she says.

Sheila's career as an executive chef is a challenge she loves, and she continues to learn new things every day. In addition to being driven, wanting to be the best, and loving what she does, she often relates her work as a chef to the many years she played soccer. "There are a lot of parallels with playing soccer for me, and being a chef was a replacement when I couldn't play anymore. I always gravitated toward the back of a restaurant because there's a lot of action in the kitchen and I liked being a part of it. There's the highs and lows and the adrenaline of working through a busy shift. You can't do it alone. So there's this teamwork thing. It just instantly clicked for me and I was hooked."

From the soccer fields of Miami, the lift lines of Breckenridge, the kitchens of Denver, to the conference rooms of DC, Sheila Lucero discovered that with hard work, determination, and following one's passions, one's life can fall into place exactly as it's meant to be.

Sheila's Favorites

Time of day: Sunset because it's gorgeous in Colorado and they always stop me in my tracks.

Time of year: Fall because of sports. I also appreciate fall more now after I went to school in Miami where there isn't a fall like there is in Colorado.

Place on Earth: The Colorado Rocky Mountains on top of a 14,000-foot mountain.

Food to prepare: Seafood.

Food to eat: Sushi.

Song: "Jigsaw Falling into Place" by Radiohead.

Quote: "Luck is not a business model." —Anthony Bourdain.

Mentors: Dave Query, owner of the Big Red F Restaurant Group, and Jamey Fader, food director, Marczyk Fine Foods.

Movie: *Goodfellas.*

Book: *Kitchen Confidential: Adventures in the Culinary Underbelly* by Anthony Bourdain.

Follow Sheila Lucero Online

Website: Jax Fish House & Oyster Bar, www.jaxfishhouse.com

Instagram: @jaxfishhouse

Twitter: @jaxlodo

Facebook: @jaxfishhouselodo

Part IV
Food for Thought

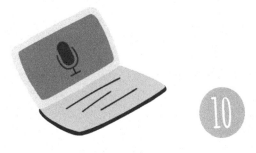

Andi Murphy:
Navajo Podcaster

Andi Murphy graduated from New Mexico State University in 2010 with a degree in journalism. She quickly landed a full-time job as an editorial assistant and features writer for the *Las Cruces Sun-News* in Las Cruces, New Mexico. It was exactly where she wanted to be.

After just a few weeks at the newspaper, Andi got a plum assignment that dramatically changed her life. The *Sun-News* also had an entertainment magazine called *Pulse* that spotlighted the food, music, and art scene of Las Cruces. The editor for *Pulse* approached Andi one day and asked if she would be interested in writing a 500-word restaurant review about Le Rendez-vous Café, a popular French café in town. The editor needed a writer on the spot because the regular food writer wasn't available.

Instantly on board, Andi replied succinctly. "Okay, cool. That sounds awesome." Although she claims she was a bit nervous to tackle the review, she grabbed her gear and was off for a mouthwatering rendezvous with journalism and food.

At the café Andi ordered a basket of bread, French onion soup, and an eye-catching piece of cake that had many chocolate and vanilla layers and a chocolate design on top. Andi took her own photo of the cake that day, which appeared alongside her copy when it was published. "I came back and wrote the review, and I think I did a pretty good job." She then landed more food assignments for *Pulse*.

With her newfound culinary niche, Andi started reviewing restaurants all over Las Cruces with a column called "Delightful Dish." She wrote about a wide range of international foods such as Afghan, Mediterranean, Asian, and Mexican. With each assignment she would talk with the restaurant owners and chefs, photograph the many dishes, and write a description with her own words. "It was my entry into the whole world of food. That's how I got started."

Andi Murphy lives in Albuquerque, New Mexico, and is an award-winning Navajo journalist, radio producer, food writer, and photographer. She hosts and produces the *Toasted Sister Podcast*, which she created in 2017. Her podcast highlights a wide range of stories about Indigenous people and foods, the Native food movement, and food sovereignty. Andi is also a radio producer for *Native America Calling* (NAC), a live radio call-in show headquartered in Albuquerque, which provides a thought-provoking national forum about key Indigenous issues related to Native communities. She also hosts *The Menu*, a NAC radio feature that explores Indigenous food and food sovereignty.

What is Indigenous Food?

Indigenous food is an integral part of Native American cuisine. The term *indigenous* means something that is native to, or comes from, a specific region on Earth. "Generally, *Indigenous* refers to those peoples with pre-existing sovereignty who were living as a community prior to contact with settler populations, most often—though not exclusively—Europeans." Indigenous food is the native food of a region that is hunted, fished, grown, harvested, prepared, and eaten there.

Native American Indigenous food is considered traditional cuisine because it has endured through time and societal changes, such as the European colonization of America. Examples of Native American Indigenous cuisine include meats such as buffalo, elk, caribou, salmon, ducks, geese, and turkeys; grains such as blue corn and wild rice; fruits such as cranberries, blackberries, grapes, and mayhaws; nuts such as pine nuts and acorns; and plants such as mushrooms and wild greens—to name a few. Three key crops of Native American cuisine include corn, beans, and squash, which are often referred to as the Three Sisters. Chef Sean Sherman (Oglala Lakota), is the author of *The Sioux Chef's Indigenous Kitchen,* a vibrant and informative book about Native American Indigenous cuisine.

Andi grew up in a tight-knit family in the small rural town of Crownpoint, New Mexico, which is located in the Navajo Nation. The Navajo Nation is a vast Native American reservation that spans more than 27,000 square miles through portions of New Mexico, Arizona, and Utah.

The town of Crownpoint is located in the dry high desert of New Mexico and surrounded by mesas, vibrant red hills, sage-colored shrubs, and juniper trees. "It's pretty green in the summer," Andi says. "But when the fall and winter come, it's gray and brown and I used to not like that." Andi wanted to live somewhere with trees and water and a beach. But over time, when she started to travel across the United States, Andi came to appreciate her homeland. "Now I really love the desert and I see the beauty of it. I can't imagine ever leaving the Southwest. It's where I belong."

Crownpoint had few stores when Andi was growing up, and she loved traveling with her family on weekends to the neighboring towns of Gallup, Farmington, or Albuquerque to buy clothes or get essentials like shampoo. "It was really fun, and sometimes we would eat at my mom and dad's one or two favorite restaurants."

Growing up, she spent a lot of time with her younger sister, Alisha, and they were very close. "I grew up kind of like the quiet, shy kid, and I really just hung out with my sister."

At Crownpoint High School, Andi says she was more or less a loner but loved playing volleyball with Alisha. "Volleyball was very special to me, and I looked forward to it every single year. I started in fifth grade and then got on the varsity high school volleyball team. I was a middle blocker and hitter because I'm pretty tall and my arms are long." Andi says her parents were always very supportive and never missed a single game whether it was at home or away.

In 2006 Andi headed to New Mexico Highlands University in Las Vegas, New Mexico, to begin her freshman year. Wanting to become a novelist, she became an English major to focus on her passion for writing.

Moving away from home was an exciting eye-opener that Andi describes as a "crash course in the rest of the world," and she began to meet a wide variety of students and teachers in class and on campus. "I started learning about other people for the first time. In Crownpoint everyone I went to school with was Navajo, and I didn't have interaction with other people other than my non-Native teachers."

After about two years at Highlands University, Andi's academic interests changed. She started to look for scholarships and found one that intrigued her. "It was a Native journalist scholarship and I think they were welcoming English majors," she explains.

Andi got the scholarship, which was with the American Indian Journalism Institute located at the University of South Dakota. Part of the AIJI scholarship meant attending an intensive two-week journalism boot camp that summer at the university. "It was exhausting but fun," she says. "We learned about the basics of journalism and multimedia journalism. It changed my mind about how I could use my passion for writing for my community and an actual career."

At the boot camp Andi also learned how Native American journalists were sought after in both Native and non-Native newsrooms. "Our voices are needed. We need to tell our own stories because we know our communities best."

The South Dakota boot camp was another important moment in Andi's life. When she returned home that summer, she began an internship with the *Farmington Daily Times* that was not too far from her hometown. "I got dumped into the newsroom and I thought, *Oh my gosh, this is such a challenging and intimidating job.*" All of a sudden she was exposed to the inner workings of how a city and municipality leaders operate as she covered various stories.

But challenging or not, Andi was determined to become a journalist. She decided to leave Highlands University and study journalism at New Mexico State University in Las

Cruces. Andi was happy that Alisha was already attending NMSU, and a few family members lived in Las Cruces.

Over the next few years she attended two more summer internships at newspapers in Great Falls, Montana, and Fargo, North Dakota. Her familiarity with the workings of a news-room continued to grow. But the hands-on internships helped Andi realize that she wanted to focus on writing colorful feature stories versus hard news pieces. "I've always wanted to be a storyteller, so I connect to feature writing and writing personal stories such as about someone who opened a little cupcake shop, or won the lottery, or survived a health crisis. Those are the stories I really like."

While attending NMSU, Andi rented a small apartment in Las Cruces where she had her own kitchen for the first time. This is where she began to teach herself to how to cook, expanding her kitchen know-how beyond the helpful advice of her mother. Andi was raised eating traditional American fare such as spaghetti, mashed potatoes and pork chops, and fried potatoes and rice. "It was really simple food because we were a very busy family. But in college I got to explore culinary freedom, and I was getting obsessed with food! So I started building my own kitchen and getting more utensils, dishes, and pots and pans."

Andi would comb through cookbooks, watch cooking shows on the Food Network, or check out food websites or instructional YouTube videos. "I learned to cook in Las Cruces, and over the years I got better and better at it by adding more spices and a lot more ingredients to my pantry."

When the food-writing beat opened up at the *Sun-News* in 2011, it was a natural fit for Andi, and she became a full-fledged feature writer and foodie. Over time Andi was recognized as the food writer for Las Cruces. She would head into restaurants and owners would spot her right away. So it made complete sense when her editor suggested she start a food blog to share her words, photos, and comedic flair on social media. *I can do this!* Andi thought.

After three years with the *Sun-News* Andi's life changed again. This time it meant moving to a new city and starting a whole new job in radio. It began when Andi attended a networking function in Las Cruces where she met the executive producer of *Native America Calling*, a national call-in radio show produced in Albuquerque.

Later, Andi learned that NAC had a job opening and she applied for it. After traveling to the studio for an interview, she was offered an associate radio producer position and was delighted. "*Native America Calling* was my opportunity to tell Native stories, which is where my passion for journalism came from."

In the summer of 2014, Andi said goodbye to Las Cruces, a town she had grown to love, and headed north to Albuquerque to start her new job in radio. She already had experience producing multimedia pieces, but now she needed to hone her broadcast skills. "I started listening to a ton more radio and a couple of podcasts, and I learned how broadcast writing is different from print. It's a little more casual and a lot shorter, and it wasn't too difficult."

And then during her Monday editorial meetings, she started to pitch story ideas—especially about Native American food. Her ideas were flowing with energy and enthusiasm, but after a while, Andi's editor asked her to expand her topics beyond food. "It was frustrating because I was learning about all these amazing chefs who were doing really cool work to revitalize Native American food," Andi says.

Fortunately, a coworker said, "Why don't you start a podcast?"

Andi wondered if it was time to do something new. "When I started producing food shows for *Native America Calling*, I noticed there was a lot of work being done all across these Native communities across the country, with chefs, farmers, individuals, entrepreneurs, and nonprofit groups. They were working to strengthen Native foodways and share knowledge."

Enter the *Toasted Sister Podcast*.

Andi worked on figuring out everything she needed to get her podcast up and running. First things first—she drew her own logo of a stalk of corn with a microphone on top. And even though Andi kept her *Toasted Sister* name from her food blog, she breathed new life into her topics with sound. Her focus would now be on the Native American food movement. "I talk with chefs and farmers and knowledge-keepers, and scientists and doctors and sometimes musicians. It's continuing my obsession with food and just realizing there's a whole lot

more behind a plate of food. There are generations of ancestors behind these foods."

Andi's first podcast episode was on January 5, 2017, with
chef Karlos Baca (Tewa, Diné, Nuche) from the Southern Ute
territory in southwestern Colorado. Karlos talked about the
value of cooking with Indigenous foods such as mushrooms,
berries, and wild greens found through foraging in nature.

Since starting the podcast, Andi has produced more than 70
episodes including interviews with chef Nephi Craig (White
Mountain Apache, Diné), "This Radical Pathway"; Sioux chef
Sean Sherman (Oglala Lakota), "Redefine North America
Food"; Dr. Elizabeth Hoover (Mohawk and Mi'kmaq), "Food
Sovereignty"; Donell Barlow (Ottawa), "Food Is Medicine";
Alisha Murphy (Navajo), "Food Stories" and "I Loved My
Trip to New Zealand"; and David Wolfman (Xaxli'p First
Nation), "Reclaiming Our Heritage One Bite at a Time."

Although she's referred to her podcast as a hobby, Andi
won first place for Radio/Podcast General Excellence for the
2019 National Native Media Awards of the Native American
Journalists Association.

Understanding Food Sovereignty

The term *sovereignty* means having control over something and being self-sufficient. There is a great deal of
food sovereignty work happening within Native American
communities today. But what does food sovereignty mean?

According to the US Food Sovereignty Alliance, "Food sovereignty is the right of peoples to healthy and culturally appropriate food produced through ecologically sound and sustainable methods, and their right to define their own food and agriculture systems. It puts the aspirations and needs of those who produce, distribute and consume food at the heart of food systems and policies rather than the demands of markets and corporations."

Andi thinks a lot about this issue. "I think the basic definition of food sovereignty is the ability for a community to feed itself."

In a 2020 interview with Kerry Diamond for the *Radio Cherry Bombe* podcast, Andi says, "Food sovereignty is reclaiming your food [and] revitalizing Indigenous food knowledge and foodways. It is also very personal too for an individual to explore their own food sovereignty, remembering the foods from your family, [and] remembering the foods from your tribe, which is something that I still like to work on myself right now."

For more information, check out the Native American Food Sovereignty Alliance website at nativefoodalliance.org.

As a Navajo and journalist, Andi is frequently interviewed by the media during the month of November about the Thanksgiving holiday, which she says can feel lopsided. "Everybody wants us and our voices in November and just kind of forgets about us the rest of the year."

She definitely has many mixed feelings about Thanksgiving. "A lot of people don't know the true history of Thanksgiving," Andi says. "It's been Americanized."

In elementary school Andi learned about what she calls a caricature version of the history of Thanksgiving. "Growing up I learned whatever other Americans learned about Pilgrims and Indians. We made a turkey hand art and we pasted our Pilgrim and Indian art projects on the walls. The real history of Native issues isn't taught in public schools."

While growing up, Andi says her family celebrated Thanksgiving, but it was never about the story of Pilgrims and Indians. It was more like a football holiday. "We're a big Green Bay Packers family. Everybody has the day off, and we all gather in Crownpoint and cook and have the delicious turkey and gravy dishes. We eat and laugh together and watch football."

She says she learned about the real history of Native issues later in life in college. "That's where I got the crash course in Native history and law and policy because my minor was Native American studies," Andi says. "Around that time I was an angry person. I think every Native person has this anger inside of them, like all the time, especially when we learn about the atrocities that happened to our own people and to other tribes across the country."

Andi says she now channels her anger into her work to keep sharing important stories. "I use all of that as fuel for the fire to keep doing what I'm doing."

In 2020, she devoted episode 70, "The Thanksgiving Episode," of her *Toasted Sister Podcast* to share more information about the true story of this day. She talked with three Wampanoag women (Chef Sherry Pocknett of Sly Fox Den Restaurant, educator Danielle Hill with Heron-Hill LLC, and Talia Landry with Mashpee TV) about Thanksgiving and how 400 years of colonization have affected their foodways since the Pilgrims first landed in New England in 1620.

Andi's Favorites

Time of day: Sundown, when the sky changes colors after the sun sets.

Time of year: Fall and winter in my Southwest desert.

Place on Earth: My kitchen.

Food: Middle Eastern, Mediterranean, and Afghan.

Podcast topic: The positive ones. I like when people talk about making change and doing good work.

Song: "Cry for Love" by Iggy Pop. (This is a really hard question! I listen to tons of music every day.)

Saying: "Let's do it!"

Inspiration: Cookbooks and food magazines.

Movie: *What's Eating Gilbert Grape?*

Books: Cookbooks from *America's Test Kitchen*.

Follow Andi Murphy Online

Podcast: toastedsisterpodcast.com

Instagram: @toastedsister

Twitter: @andimurphy

11

Abby Fuller: Foodie Filmmaker

After graduating from film school, Abby Fuller worked for years to hone her directing skills and make a difference in the world. Her area of expertise was documentary filmmaking, and her passion was food.

When Abby landed a coveted assignment in 2015 to direct an episode for the popular documentary TV series *Chef's Table*, she was so excited. At the time she was the youngest and only female director to be hired for this Emmy-nominated Netflix series.

That September Abby traveled far from home to direct a 50-minute *Chef's Table* episode about self-taught cook Ana Roš, who became the acclaimed chef at the Hiša Franko restaurant in the European country of Slovenia. "I'd heard about

Slovenia, but I pretty much knew nothing about it," Abby says. "I didn't know what the climate was like, or the topography, or the food."

Wanting to get a lay of the land, Abby set out a week before the shoot to check out the stunning Soča Valley in Northern Slovenia where the Hiša Franko restaurant was located. "I rented a car and drove through the countryside, and it was unbelievably beautiful." Abby rafted down turquoise-colored rivers, foraged for mushrooms in misty woods, and hiked into the mountains to learn about cheesemaking. It gave her an important sense of her surroundings.

But when her crew arrived and started to film the very first interview with Ana Roš, Abby was almost stopped in her tracks. The interview was scheduled to last three hours, but Abby said nothing seemed to be going right—Ana's makeup looked too formal, filming inside the restaurant fell flat, and Abby's interview with Ana in English wasn't working. "About 30 minutes into the interview, I just said, 'CUT!'" Abby says. "The whole crew was looking at me and asking, 'What's going on?'"

Abby had to think fast on her feet and switch direction. She moved the crew from the dining area into the kitchen and called for a camera lens change so cinematographer Adam Bricker could start filming Ana's cooking. "I felt like the most important thing in that moment was that I seemed like I had a plan."

The next day her producer hired a translator so Ana could speak in her native Slovenian language. Abby also decided to film Ana outdoors for a more rustic feel to the footage. And with some guidance with hair and makeup, Ana's appearance took on a more natural look. "I just wanted to change everything about it to make it feel more like Ana," Abby says. "I had to be confident in what I was doing."

And she was.

Abby Fuller is a director of documentary films, and her unique storytelling skills often revolve around food-related topics. She directed *The Freshman Class* series for the Cooking Channel, and five episodes of *Chef's Table* for Netflix. In addition, Abby directed the 2015 feature documentary *Do You Dream in Color?* about four blind high school students, as well as the 2020 documentary *Shepherd's Song* about restorative grazing. She has also directed documentaries for MTV, SundanceTV, National Geographic, Apple TV+, and Disney. Today Abby lives on APD Farm in Northern Virginia and continues to work on film projects.

Chef's Table

Chef's Table premiered in April 2015, and was an original documentary television series brought to viewers via Netflix, a US subscription-based streaming service. The series, produced by Boardwalk Pictures and Supper Club, was created and developed by film director David Gelb, who directed the 2011 documentary, *Jiro Dreams of Sushi*.

Chef's Table, which has been renewed for many seasons over the years, highlights stories about the lives and work of acclaimed chefs from all over the world in countries such as Mexico, Thailand, Germany, India, Slovenia, the United States, Italy, and Japan, to name a few. Beautiful cinematography and music help bring to life a unique presentation and personal story for each chef.

The show has garnered many awards over the years including a number of James Beard Awards and Emmy Award nominations.

Abby grew up in Latham, New York, which is a small suburb of Albany. Her neighborhood wasn't exactly her cup of tea. "Latham was the epitome of suburban mediocrity," Abby says. "There was always the thought of, *There's got to be something better than this.*"

Nonetheless, there were many fun activities in her "cookie cutter" childhood world. "My best friends and I used to ride our bikes around, and there was still farmland in a five- to ten-minute bike ride. We used to go and jump on hay bales and pick berries and explore the woods."

Early on she says she tried a lot of different sports growing up but was always way more drawn to art and filmmaking. "I loved making movies from a very young age, and I was always recruiting friends and kids from the neighborhood."

Her passion for cinematography endured. In high school she was active in various cinematography clubs and says she was sometimes the only girl in the club. "I wasn't the most popular kid because I was the nerdy kid with a video camera," she laughs. "I was thrilled that I could actually edit something together, and I remember staying after school editing until I was kicked out."

Her early memories of food include family meals with her parents and older brother. "I ate a typical 1990s American diet and a lot of things came in boxes, like Cheerios and Frosted Flakes. My mom cooked for convenience and would make things like chicken breasts and cheesy broccoli in the microwave. Or we'd get Chinese takeout."

She says her parents weren't exactly foodies. "One of my friend's family had a garden with peppers and strawberries, but my parents were not focused on gardening or cooking."

When Abby was a teen, however, she and her mom loved to watch Food Network shows together with celebrity cooks such as Ina Garten, Rachael Ray, Tyler Florence, and Giada De Laurentiis. These shows introduced Abby to a whole new culinary world, and it was a fun and educational thing to do with her mom.

Abby's life changed big time when she was a senior in high school. At 16, she traveled to the small town of Orotina, Costa Rica, as an exchange student with the American Field Service. This bold adventure ignited Abby's interest in different types of cultures and food. "Not only did I make friends with all the Costa Ricans in my small town," she says, "a lot of my friends were other exchange students from Italy, Japan, Thailand, Norway, Australia, and Germany."

She was also exposed to delicious new dishes such as ceviche (marinated raw fish) and *arroz con mariscos* (rice with seafood), which she savored. Abby says that Orotina was called the Ciudad de las Frutas (fruit city) because so many tropical fruits were grown there. "In the morning I would have fresh juice made from carrots, guanábana, mango, or coconut water. It was a daily part of life that was so exciting because you could never have that in Albany."

Abby also met people from around the world during her seven months in Costa Rica. "I got this infusion of not only being an expat, but I also learned there were so many different ways to approach food, life, and different cultures. It was a really formative experience."

After returning home, Abby started film school at the University of Southern California in Los Angeles. The school was near the heart of Hollywood, and Abby started taking classes in cinema history, production, screen writing, and film theory.

"Getting to know L.A. was kind of a slow burn," she says. "But I was suddenly immersed with really interesting, bright, sharp, ambitious, creative, and funny people from all over. That was so stimulating to me—to meet people who had talent and wanted to create. I was really filled up getting to know the stories of people, which is why I love documentaries."

The Art of Directing Nonfiction Media

Many people have high hopes of directing a fictional blockbuster movie or award-winning television series. The competition can be steep, and it can take years to move up the Hollywood directorial ladder. It's good to know there are many potential careers that involve directing nonfiction stories about people and events that are based in real life. Nonfiction television is often referred to as factual or reality-based TV, while a nonfiction film is called a documentary.

A lot of work goes into producing nonfiction media, and the director has a huge responsibility in bringing to life the final production of a piece. The director is responsible for the overall vision in how a story will come together.

"A director is really the chief creative voice in a film, documentary, or commercial," Abby says. "They are the person who is really in charge of the vision, tone, style, and story. The director works with different talented people that we call department heads, such as the cinematographer, art director, editor, and composer, depending on the subject."

Cinema verité, which means "truthful cinema," is a style of filmmaking that's often used with different kinds of nonfiction productions. It's associated with how a cinematographer captures a scene on camera so that it looks realistic to viewers. Some of the basic techniques of this type of filmmaking include using a handheld camera, filming nonprofessional actors where they work or live, working without a script or screenplay, and the use of natural lighting.

An example of the cinema verité technique would be a cinematographer filming foods prepared and cooked in a kitchen setting with a handheld camera.

After graduating from USC in 2008 with a BA in cinematic arts, Abby pounded the pavement to find work in her field. Over the next few years, she was hired as a writer and story producer for two production companies in the L.A. area.

She moved to New York City in 2012 and landed a job producing two episodes for the MTV *True Life* series.

Abby loved what she was doing, but there were big challenges. She quickly realized she needed to find a decent-paying job to pay Big Apple rent. She had previously turned to a colleague for advice on how to get ahead in the competitive world of documentary filmmaking. He told her that instead of saying she was open to working on anything available—she needed to be very specific about finding something she was truly passionate about.

Abby did some soul searching and knew her passion was all about food. It was definitely an interest that had emerged years earlier when she was in college. "Suddenly this explosion of food happened in L.A., and there was this whole new world I didn't know about."

An avid storyteller, Abby decided to put pencil to paper, and she and her college friend Shevin started to write a food blog called *Foodie Fridays*. The blog profiled eateries in Southern California with plenty of photos of delectable dishes. To write the blog posts, the two friends spent a lot of time dining in different restaurants throughout L.A.

But now in New York, Abby decided to take her colleague's advice. She started to let people know that she was super interested in working on food-related projects for television.

This was a smart move because it wasn't long before the producers of *True Life* realized Abby would be a perfect fit to direct and produce a new TV series called *The Freshman Class* for the Cooking Channel. The series featured first-year students in culinary school, and Abby moved to Baton Rouge, Louisiana, to work on the show's first season in 2013.

"Suddenly I was immersed into the South in Louisiana. So it was spending time in Cajun country in the bayou, listening to the music of New Orleans, and eating étouffée (shellfish over rice) and alligator. It was an incredible culture, and I had a great time."

Over the next few years Abby worked on a number of shows in California and New York and directed the feature film, *Do You Dream in Color?* She also directed the TV comedy series, *That's Racist with Mike Epps,* which was produced by Boardwalk Pictures in Santa Monica, California.

Fortunately, Abby was at the right place at the right time. Boardwalk Pictures was also producing the first season of *Chef's Table* at her exact location.

The president of Boardwalk Pictures noticed how hard Abby worked on the Mike Epps comedy series and wanted her to stay on. He asked Abby what she'd like to do next. It was a no-brainer. "I basically said, 'I want to direct *Chef's Table.*'" Then she added, "I have relevant experience, a feature film, and I've directed commercials and shows that highlight food, travel, and chefs. Plus, you don't have any women in any key positions on the show. It could only benefit you guys to diversify your storytelling."

Abby's points were well taken. She then had lunch with show creator, David Gelb, and was soon hired to direct the *Chef's Table* episode about Ana Roš.

There was a lot on her plate during the early days of the series, and she had to figure out many things by herself. "It was like, 'Here's the email about the chef—go and make the episode,'" Abby says. "There was no show bible, no researcher, and no real support person for pre-production." Fortunately her years of film experience made all the difference.

"I felt like, okay, they're either giving me just enough rope to hang myself because I don't feel like I have a ton of support, or . . . this is the most incredible opportunity to have such full trust and creative control where no one's trying to micromanage the creative process."

On top of everything, once Abby was in Slovenia, she wasn't able to film Ana right away because Ana was out of town. So Ana's husband, Valter, showed Abby the sights on his motorcycle. "We went up to meet with these old men in the mountains, and I started milking cows and tasting cheese and wine." Abby then cleverly incorporated these adventures into Ana's story.

The episode about Ana Roš was a vibrant success, and Abby went on to direct more *Chef's Table* episodes including shows about Tim Raue in Berlin, Cristina Martinez in Philadelphia, and Mashama Bailey in Savannah, Georgia. In 2021 she was assigned to direct an episode about Yoshihiro Imai in Kyoto, Japan.

But years earlier, in 2015, Abby's first *Chef's Table* episode with Ana was a huge eye-opener and a life-changer. "I had hit a point where I realized L.A. never truly felt like home and I could never see myself there forever. The Slovenia experience was a bit of a spark."

Being in the Soča Valley planted a seed in her mind that country living might be right for her. Abby explained that after growing up in a suburban neighborhood she was convinced she needed to make a living in a big city. She thought that living in a rural area meant one's life would be devoid of opportunity and ambition.

Meeting Ana helped alter this urban mindset. "I saw that somebody like Ana, who was living out in the country, foraging and eating fresh food from the garden, and living in the mountains, also had this really amazing career. She had community and nature, and she also had her art."

From this point on, Abby's life started to change. Less than a year later she was introduced to her husband, Matt Rales, through mutual friends. Abby learned that Matt had purchased a 1,500-acre farm in Northern Virginia in 2016. The farm is now a regenerative cattle farm called APD Farm, which stands for Another Perfect Day.

Regenerative farming focuses on improving ecosystem function, soil health, and creating a biodiverse wildlife habitat on a farm. The guiding principle is to create agriculture that mimics nature.

But before meeting in person, Abby and Matt talked on the phone for nearly four months. Abby says their conversations usually centered around the farm or what they were eating that day. Once they met, they clicked, and Abby eventually moved to the farm to be with Matt.

Abby and Matt married in 2019 with a marriage ceremony in Kenya, Africa, and a reception on the farm. "Living in a way that feels deeply connected to the land and the seasons and knowing where my food comes from has been a really meaningful and profound opening in my life," she says. "My passion for food first started with what I was being served on a plate in a restaurant, and I enjoyed that so much. But I've gone back now to where it all begins, and it's pretty special to live among animals and nature."

Living on a farm seems like an ideal location for Abby's career. She now conducts her documentary filmmaking from this rural home base, and she still travels the world in search of amazing stories. "I've always loved the art and craft of filmmaking, and I'm so filled up that I get to learn people's stories," she says. "I really care about them, and it's a huge responsibility and privilege to do right by them."

Abby's Favorites

Time of day: Morning, with coffee.

Time of year: Fall. October is usually the best as fall starts to set in.

Place on Earth: Hard to choose just one! Perhaps Mahale Mountain National Park in Tanzania.

Food to film: Cheesemaking.

Food to eat: Sushi.

Music: Right now, I've been listening to some throwbacks from the Neville Brothers and Bon Iver.

Saying: "Anything Is Possible."

Movie: Impossible to choose one. I like French New Wave, Latin American cinema, '90s Hollywood films, and of course many documentaries.

Books: *Ishmael* by David Quinn is a classic. I love *Blood, Bones & Butter: The Inadvertent Education of a Reluctant Chef* by Gabrielle Hamilton. I just finished and loved

Between Two Kingdoms: A Memoir of a Life Interrupted by Suleika Jaouad and was left totally speechless.

Follow Abby Fuller Online

Websites: abby-fuller.com; www.nonfictionunlimited .com/directors/abigail-fuller/

Instagram: @abrafever

Jocelyn Ramirez:
Vegan Cookbook Author

It was a long drive home from the doctor's office in 2015 when Jocelyn Ramirez learned her father's cancer had returned. Her heart sank, but she wasn't about to take the devastating news sitting down. Jocelyn wanted to help her dad in the best way she knew how by making healthy food for him.

She quickly talked with her parents about finding new meal plans and healthier ways to eat. "I had already been focusing on eating in a healthier way for myself and I encouraged them to eat in a different way too. I cleaned out their kitchen and all their cupboards and we just started fresh," Jocelyn says.

Then her imagination kicked in, and she began creating delicious superfood smoothies for her dad. These plant-based smoothies were chock-full of nutritious foods such as fresh fruit, almond milk, and kale.

In time Jocelyn's dad felt better, and soon friends and family members were asking for her special superfood smoothies. This was her incentive to take her smoothie on the road. Jocelyn began to set up booths in various farmers markets in her hometown, where she could make the healthy drinks on the spot for eager customers.

This new interest in becoming a purveyor of healthy food started her on a fulfilling journey that changed her life. And she's never looked back.

Jocelyn Ramirez is the founder of the Los Angeles–based food company, Todo Verde, and she is the author of the cookbook, *La Vida Verde: Plant-Based Mexican Cooking with Authentic Flavor*. As a plant-based eater Jocelyn strives to eat in a way she believes is healthy, is caring and considerate of animals, and helps sustain Earth's environment.

Jocelyn was born in East Los Angeles and grew up in the nearby community of South Gate. "They're both predominantly Latin-mixed neighborhoods," she says.

Amid lemon, lime, and avocado trees, rose-colored bougainvillea flowers, single-family bungalows, apartment complexes, fast-food stands, and car dealerships, South Gate was a busy urban environment. Jocelyn's neighborhood was always bustling with activity and offered what she calls a "very family-centric culture."

Her parents immigrated to the United States years before she was born—her mother is from Mexico and her father is from Ecuador. While growing up in South Gate, Jocelyn's parents worked full time and were often at work when she and her brother, who is seven years older, got home from school.

As children they needed to fend for themselves after school, which meant finding afternoon snacks. "My brother and I were latchkey kids like many of the other kids in the neighborhood. We would often pick up food somewhere, or I would come home and make a cup of noodles. We relied on a lot of junky processed foods, and I think for my family and a lot of people who immigrated here, they probably didn't know the nature of processed foods and what they could do to somebody down the line."

The Lack of Food Equity

Food equity means having equal amounts of nutritious and accessible food for everyone in a community. But that's not often the case, and many people have trouble finding and consuming healthy foods. Different terms have been coined over the years to describe a community's lack of adequate, available, affordable, and nutritious food to grow, buy, and eat for all.

A *food desert* describes a community that doesn't have enough healthy food (such as fruits and vegetables) that is readily available to buy in grocery stores. A *food swamp* is a community that has more unhealthy fast-food options, such as fast-food outlets, convenience stores, or liquor stores, than nutritious food options. A *food mirage* is a community that has healthy food in grocery stores or restaurants but it's expensive and not affordable for everyone to buy. *Food apartheid* takes into account race, income, and geography, and describes the inequitable situation when a community has access to nutritious food for some but not all of its community members.

It's helpful to think about how we can use food equity terms effectively. According to Nina Sevilla's NRDC (Natural Resources Defense Council) blog post, "Food Apartheid: Racialized Access to Healthy Affordable Food," "The language we use to describe the issues can inspire solutions, so we should follow the lead of food justice leaders who urge us to reconceptualize 'food deserts' as 'food apartheid' by focusing on creating food sovereignty through community-driven solutions and systemic change."

When Jocelyn's mother cooked for the family, she would often prepare delicious Mexican stews called *guisados*. She also made quesadillas stuffed with meat or cheese, *nopales*, an edible cactus, or rice and beans. But her mom wasn't that keen on cooking, and her father often didn't care for the spicy Mexican foods she prepared. "Overall, she cooked to survive," Jocelyn says.

Jocelyn's true food mentor was her beloved maternal grandmother, Beatriz, she affectionately called Abuelita. Her grandmother lived about an hour from South Gate in the San Fernando Valley neighborhood of Canoga Park. Her grandparents' home had a large yard and garden. They were skilled farmers and had previously lived on a ranch in Mexico before moving to the United States. "When they came here they brought that farming know-how and grew tons of their own food from tomatoes to chilies," Jocelyn says. "They had fig trees, corn, sugar cane—you name it, they grew it."

The Canoga Park home was also a fun entertainment hub with a kitchen bursting with flavors and fragrances. "That's where all the parties were. Birthdays. Baptisms. Everybody went to Canoga Park. My grandmother would cook tons of food with all my aunts. The dish I loved most was called *sopa de fideo,* which is a Mexican noodle soup. When I'd go for a visit Grandma would already have it on the stove because she knew I loved it."

At their grandparents' home, it was common for Jocelyn's extended family to feast on savory dishes, such as carne asada, which is a grilled Mexican beef dish. And on some occasions, family members would bring home a pig or goat, slaughter it, and then stew it in lard or birria broth in the backyard.

Jocelyn's grandmother also taught her how to cook. "For the holidays she would gather us and teach everybody how to make something," Jocelyn says.

When Jocelyn got older she decided to take up a musical instrument. Her father played guitar and sang, and Jocelyn became passionate about learning to play the accordion. But this new interest wasn't meant to be. "It was just too hard and I couldn't do it."

Jocelyn did have a lot of success playing sports in school and at home. "In our neighborhood, basketball was a huge thing." She says many neighborhood kids played basketball at her home because she had a big backyard and a basketball court.

Jocelyn was good at many sports through middle and high school including volleyball and softball. "I'm a fast runner, but softball was probably my best sport. I was a home run hitter."

When it was time for college, Jocelyn enrolled at Woodbury University, which was about a half hour north of her home. "I initially wanted to study architecture because I was good at math and science and I loved physics." But Jocelyn realized she was more interested in learning about design and marketing and eventually earned a bachelor of fine arts at the university. It was a fulfilling time in her life, and in addition to her studies, she became very involved in the school's student leadership program.

She also began to cook for friends in her dorm. And she loved watching Food Network cooking shows on TV. "I did learn a lot from watching these shows whether they were Mexican or not. I always liked the show *Chopped*."

After graduating she started a small marketing company in Los Angeles with a few friends to help clients with business needs such as creating logos or websites. But in a few years Jocelyn returned to Woodbury for a master's degree in business. During her master's she worked as an academic counselor at the school and also began teaching courses in social justice and community engagement. At home she enjoyed making and selling jewelry. She had a busy, happy, and creative life.

But during her graduate studies at Woodbury, Jocelyn started having health problems. She was in her twenties and discovered she had nodules on her thyroid. Although her doctors suggested surgery to correct her thyroid problem, Jocelyn was eager to find alternative solutions. This prompted her to make major life changes. "I started to shift the way that I ate, and I started getting more into yoga," she says. "I thought, what if I try to eliminate my meat consumption because I ate meat all the time, especially street tacos. I started to notice that when I ate those things my eyes got really irritated. I just didn't feel good."

As Jocelyn slowly phased out meat consumption, she says her family and friends were all shocked. She was the last person they ever expected to go vegetarian. And then, over the next few years, Jocelyn decided to adopt a more plant-based diet to see if that would help her with her thyroid nodules.

Although she still has nodules, she says they're shrinking. "It's still a work in progress," Jocelyn explains. "It's a really nice feeling to know that intuitively my body is in charge and I just have to make wise decisions for it in terms of what I put into my body."

As Jocelyn began to eat fewer animal-based foods, she wanted to learn more about nutrition and how to eat. Jocelyn took a brief culinary training program with plant-based celebrity chef Matthew Kenney. She also attended an Indigenous veganism workshop led by the culinary anthropologist Claudia Serrato in the East Los Angeles area.

At the time Jocelyn was still vegetarian, but wanted to learn more about a plant-based diet. "Claudia connected feminism to veganism, and that part really got to me. From that day forward, I chose to become vegan."

Understanding Veganism

It's easy to see the first three letters of the word *vegetable* in the term *vegan*. Although some humans have avoided eating animal products for centuries, the concept of veganism started decades ago. The Vegan Society was cofounded by animal rights activist and woodworker Donald Watson in 1944 in England, when he, his wife, and a few other individuals met to discuss nondairy vegetarianism. Vegetarians do not eat meat, poultry, fish, or seafood, but they may choose to consume dairy products such as eggs, milk, or cheese.

People who choose the vegan diet do not eat or drink any animal products including meat, poultry, fish, seafood, eggs, milk, cheese, or honey. In addition, they often will not use or wear products made from animals such as leather, wool, or silk. They even avoid soaps made from animal products. Those who adopt a vegan diet derive their nutrition and energy from plant-based foods including fruits, vegetables, nuts, seeds, legumes, vegetable oils, and plant-based milks, cheeses, and yogurts. Part of a person's desire to become vegetarian or vegan stems from wanting to feel healthier, caring about animals, and wanting to protect and sustain the environment.

Jocelyn also wanted to help her family members. "As my immediate family started to deal with more health issues such as cancer and diabetes, I was trying to encourage them and share what I had learned. That was the foundation of the transition for us, especially when my father's cancer returned." And that's when she began making her nutritious superfood smoothies. "A superfood is an ultra-nutrient-dense food that provides a lot of the things your body needs in a small quantity," Jocelyn says. "A few examples would be avocado, kale, and almonds."

Once she realized her superfood smoothies were helping her dad feel better, she realized other people might like them too. And then her dad told her something that changed her life. "Working with food seems to be your thing," he said. "You should open a restaurant one day."

Jocelyn knew she wasn't ready to open a restaurant because she had limited experience in the culinary field. But the food industry was exciting to her, and she had found a new passion. She just needed to move forward in a logical way that she could handle.

After stepping away from her career at Woodbury University, she put her business acumen to work and created a culinary business plan. This process took her nearly one year. She then formed a company she named Todo Verde, created a vibrant logo, and trademarked the name.

She also needed to taste test her smoothies to make sure they were yummy and had the right consistency. Her friends and family members eagerly stepped in to be her smoothie focus group.

Next move? Jocelyn started to sell her smoothies at local farmers markets. "We would come in and set up a generator and plug in the blenders next to a three-compartment sink. I would go around to other vendors and buy kale or strawberries or whatever ingredients I needed."

Jocelyn also sold traditional Mexican drinks, agua frescas, at her stand. These popular cold drinks were made by blending fruit and water, using combinations such as strawberries and rose water with pure maple syrup (or piloncillo syrup) and chia seeds.

Jocelyn's Superfood Smoothie

For a delicious and nutritious Todo Verde smoothie, blend the following ingredients in a blender to make one 16-ounce serving. You can also add fresh fruit such as strawberries if you like.

¼ Hass avocado (pitted and peeled)

1 dinosaur kale leaf

12 ounces of unsweetened almond milk

1 teaspoon of maca root powder

3 whole dates (pitted)

4 ounces of ice

Note: Maca root is a vegetable that's found in the Andes Mountains of Peru. It comes from the mustard plant family and can be ground into a powder. Jocelyn says maca root can help balance hormones and give a person energy.

About a year and a half after selling her popular sweet drinks at farmers markets, Jocelyn decided to expand Todo Verde. Her next stage was to create a savory catering business. She and her staff, including her mother, found a commercial kitchen in a centrally located building in downtown Los Angeles.

Once they were in the new kitchen, she and her Todo Verde team began making and catering plant-based foods such as jackfruit carnitas tacos topped with cashew cream and heart of palm ceviche. "Todo Verde catered everything from weddings to nonprofit meetings and conferences," she says. Jocelyn also set up a booth to sell food at a weekly event called Smorgasburg, which is a large open-air food market in downtown Los Angeles.

Her business was truly flourishing.

Part of Jocelyn's success had to do with her ability to market and promote her plant-based food products. "A lot of it was word of mouth or people following our social media and liking the photos and promoting us through that avenue," she says. "We also received a good amount of press."

One morning Jocelyn got a big surprise. She turned on her computer to find an email from an editor at Page Street Publishing in Massachusetts. Page Street had been following Jocelyn's work on social media, and they were interested in having her write a plant-based cookbook. Jocelyn was so happy because writing a cookbook had been on her to-do list for a long time.

After talking with the editor, Jocelyn was asked to send in a few recipe samples, which the publisher then tested. Once Jocelyn got the green light to move ahead, she titled her book *La Vida Verde: Plant-Based Mexican Cooking with Authentic Flavor*. Next, she wrote a table of contents featuring about 60 recipes. Writing the cookbook took nearly one year, and her friends became her taste testers to help tweak her recipes.

Once her manuscript was complete Jocelyn organized a week-long photo shoot with a food photographer who was a good friend. Jocelyn prepared all the food, and thankfully she had help from a Todo Verde chef. She also set up all the tabletops and plated all the dishes. "I was in beast mode that week," Jocelyn laughs.

Things were going well, but huge unexpected challenges were right around the corner. Just as her cookbook was about to be launched in April 2020, her happiness took an unexpected and difficult turn. Suddenly COVID-19 was surging, and people went into lockdown and stores and restaurants started to close. "The cookbook was coming out," Jocelyn says. "And all anyone cared about was COVID!"

Fortunately, despite everything, Jocelyn's cookbook was very well received. "It was a happy moment for a lot of people." *Los Angeles Times* restaurant critic Bill Addison came over to her home and picked up one of the cookbooks. He then featured Jocelyn's book in an article titled "12 Cookbooks That Refresh the Spirit and Inspire in the Kitchen," which was a big plus.

Because so many people started to cook at home during the pandemic, Jocelyn began producing online cooking classes from her kitchen with recipes from her book. "We'd all meet up on Zoom and cook the same meal together," she says. She also produced many YouTube videos featuring her plant-based recipes.

From academia to the culinary field, Jocelyn's passion for her work continues to grow with each new day. "What I love most about my work is being able to feed people who may have lost touch with their cultural cuisine. It's almost like I'm taking care of them."

And her advice for young people wanting to write a cookbook? "The most important thing is that the food has to be delicious. And I'd suggest, especially for people of color, to try to tell the story of who you are. It's not just about the food—it's culture. It's history."

In the summer of 2021, Jocelyn won the bid to be the concessions food vendor for the acclaimed John Anson Ford Amphitheatre in Los Angeles. At The Ford she offers her many plant-based Mexican dishes to hungry theater attendees.

And her future looks spicy. Jocelyn has also created a line of Todo Verde seasoning that will be sold online and in stores.

Her seasoning complements many of her plant-based recipes with culturally relevant flavors.

Jocelyn's Favorites

Time of day: Dusk during the magic hours of sunset.

Time of year: I'm a Leo and July baby. So this is a time of celebration and fun for me.

Place on Earth: I love the sounds, smells, and food of Mexico.

Food to cook: Mexican plant-based dishes.

Food to eat: Noodles.

Motto: "I'm a student of life, keep learning."

Mentors: My beloved Abuelita Beatriz Alvarez Del-Real and culinary anthropologist Claudia Serrato.

Book: *The Untethered Soul: The Journey Beyond Yourself* by Michael A. Singer.

Follow Jocelyn Ramirez Online

Website: www.todoverde.org

Instagram: @todoverde

Twitter: @TodoVerdeLA

Facebook: Todo Verde

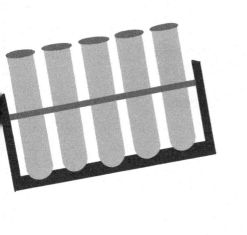

Part V
Science and Food

13

Dr. Takiyah Sirmons: NASA Food Scientist

Every day as humans go about their lives, the International Space Station (ISS) orbits our planet at a whopping 17,500 miles per hour. Round and round it goes, about 16 times in 24 hours, as the ISS astronauts expend a great deal of energy conducting science experiments, observing Earth, and exercising. All this very high-altitude work creates quite an appetite for the in-space crew.

Meanwhile, down on Earth in Houston, Texas, NASA food scientist Dr. Takiyah Sirmons is busy making sure the astronauts have nutritious foods to eat day in and day out. Her work requires a unique blend of science, culinary skills, and nutrition to create space foods that are truly out of this world.

One of the first foods Takiyah developed at NASA was a high-calorie breakfast bar. "This was my first NASA product development project," she says. "It was a little intimidating because I had never worked with breakfast bars, let alone bars for space, and I had to figure out a sensible way to tackle it. I remembered the saying, 'If you don't know where to start, just start somewhere.'" And that's exactly what she did.

But it wasn't easy, because the breakfast bars had all sorts of crucial requirements. They needed to be very high in calories, last a long time, and be compact. "And oh, by the way," Takiyah adds, "the crew had to enjoy the flavor!"

Breakfast bars, also called meal replacement bars, need to be about the same number of calories as a typical breakfast and are designed to replace breakfast foods such as eggs, sausage, potatoes, or cereal. Takiyah says she had to figure out how to make the bar before diving into the science of producing it. She first made a batch of five different flavors including jalapeno-nut, barbecue, orange-cranberry, ginger-vanilla, and banana-nut. Each bar was about the size of two smartphones stacked one on top of another. After taste testing the bars, Takiyah says her food science team liked the jalapeno-nut and barbecue best. Her favorite was the ginger-vanilla bar.

"It took me about four months to come up with the concepts and maybe two additional months to find the equipment to actually produce the bars," she says. "I liked this project because it challenged me to think outside the box, and I actually fell in love with the process."

Takiyah Sirmons has a PhD in food science and technology from Virginia Polytechnic Institute and State University in Blacksburg, Virginia. Today, as a NASA food scientist, she creates food for astronauts at the Space Food Systems Laboratory at NASA's Johnson Space Center in Houston, Texas.

Takiyah was born in Oxon Hill, Maryland, which is a suburb of Washington, DC, that's not far from the Potomac River and the National Harbor. "It's hustle and bustle there with lots of people, movement, and public transportation," she says.

Growing up, Takiyah was always into pop music and says her older brother was into art. In high school she joined the US Air Force JROTC (Junior Reserve Officers' Training Corps), which was a big part of her life as a teen, especially when she joined the school's JROTC competition drill team. "It was the most fun I ever had, and I didn't even think about the discipline and exercise that I was getting. My teammates were my family, and it taught me to stick with something even when it's difficult."

Every summer her mom signed her up for precollege science programs at universities across the country. Takiyah traveled to schools in Kentucky, North Carolina, and Iowa, and learned about many science-based research projects in food and agriculture—everything from honeybees to plant pathology.

When she attended a summer program at North Carolina Agriculture and Technical State University, she found her true calling. "I had an internship in food microbiology, and we looked at how you make cheese. This was the most interesting thing I had ever done, and I knew I wanted to be in food science."

After graduating from high school in 2004, Takiyah enrolled in the Department of Food Science and Human Nutrition at Iowa State University in Ames, Iowa. But moving to Iowa was very different from living in DC. "It was the shock of a lifetime," she says. "I did a lot of growing up during my years there because I was pushed so far out of my comfort zone. It exposed me to so much, and that's where I think I developed the mindset that I can do anything."

From Iowa, Takiyah then traveled to Virginia to pursue her doctorate degree in food science and technology at Virginia Tech.

In 2012, after earning her doctorate, Takiyah moved to Omaha, Nebraska, for her first job in her field. She was hired as a food scientist to work on the Chef Boyardee canned pasta line for ConAgra Foods (now Conagra Brands). "I remember thinking, man I used to eat this when I was a kid," she laughs.

At ConAgra, Takiyah donned her lab coat and was suddenly on a crash course in food product development. "I don't think

I would have gotten that type of experience, dare I say, anywhere else."

After one year in Omaha, change was on the horizon again when Takiyah and her fiancé moved to Houston. Now 27 years old, Takiyah looked for a new job. When a position for a NASA food scientist popped up online, she was surprised. "I'm looking at the ad thinking this can't be real. Is this some kind of joke?" But after reading the job requirements Takiyah realized her background was a good fit and she promptly sent in her résumé.

In a few weeks Takiyah was offered the job, and a new stage of her life was about to launch. "I joined NASA as a young scientist," she says. "I remember waking up the morning of my first day around 4:00 AM, just so excited I couldn't sleep. I was up and dressed two hours before I needed to go in."

Her first hours at NASA's Johnson Space Center were definitely not run of the mill. "When you arrive at the Johnson Space Center, it's not like a food company where someone from human resources greets you and walks you directly to your desk," she says. "At JSC you first go to a guard check-in post, and they direct you to security. Then you go through an entire badging process. And then someone from your lab has to escort you on-site."

Today, when Takiyah goes to work, she heads to Building 17 where NASA's Space Food Systems Laboratory is located. Building 17 is directly across the parking lot from Mission Control. "In Mission Control we can stand in a viewing deck and see all the monitors as they track the location of the International Space Station."

In the laboratory where Takiyah works, the walls and floors are a pristine white, the counters are stainless steel, the ovens are large scale, and everything needs to be incredibly clean with no dust or particles floating around.

Although some people may wonder if Takiyah is a space-age chef, she is first and foremost a scientist. As part of NASA's Advanced Food Technology division, she conducts research about the chemistry, microbiology, and composition of space food every day.

Takiyah has many tasks in this high-tech culinary process. She is responsible for figuring out how to make the food as well as standardizing the processing steps. She needs to know how long a food is cooked, at what temperature, and how a food is mixed for consistency. She also monitors the food while it's being cooked to make sure that it's produced in a safe and consistent manner.

A scientific approach to making space food is crucial, and everything needs to be precise. The weight and size of food items matter because there's only so much room on the spacecraft for storage. Plus, there's always the concern for a food item's shelf life that determines how long it can last in space and still be safe to eat.

For all these reasons, space food ingredients need to be measured, weighed, and then turned into scientific formulas. Weight matters. If Takiyah uses a recipe that calls for three tablespoons of butter, she needs to figure out how much three tablespoons of butter weighs. "Something may start from a recipe," she says. "But when it's all said and done, it's turned into a formula."

Takiyah says the process of converting a recipe into a formula is called "benchtop development," which might be compared to countertop cooking at home. She finds inspiration for different space foods from family recipes, food websites, or TV cooking shows. If Takiyah finds a recipe she wants to try, she'll make the formula a few times to adjust the ingredients. Then she'll increase it. "Instead of making three servings, I make maybe 30 servings to see how it translates to our equipment. And from there it goes into production. So you start small, and you make it bigger, bigger, and bigger. And it has to be produced in a manner that's safe."

A lot goes on in the space food lab, and there are many people who help create space food. Some individuals head to the store to buy large amounts of ingredients, such as a cartful of blueberries. "The comments you get are hilarious," Takiyah laughs. "At the checkout people might say, 'Are you prepping for doomsday?'"

But who actually makes the food? Processing technicians turn Takiyah's formulas into actual food products; many have been with NASA for a long time. Once the food is cooked, the technicians make the food ready for space. This means food needs to be freeze-dried or thermostabilized before it is placed into packages the astronauts will use on the spacecraft.

The Yum Factor in Space

Space food has come a long way since the early "tube and cube" days of spaceflight when foods were compacted into bite-size cubes or squished into containers that looked like toothpaste tubes.

Today space food is a lot more palatable and nutritious, thanks to innovative scientists and technologists who create a wide variety of MRE (Meals Ready to Eat) items. Astronauts can choose from hundreds of prepackaged foods such as scrambled eggs, lasagna, meat loaf, Turkish fish stew, butternut squash, lentil soup, shrimp fried rice, macaroni and cheese, cookies, pudding, berry cobbler, and chocolate pudding cake. The food needs to taste good, be safe to eat, and travel well in space.

At various times through the year, resupply cargo spacecraft such as the SpaceX Dragon transport food from Earth to the ISS and then bring back waste. During these cargo shipments, astronauts sometimes request fresh fruits and vegetables, such as fresh oranges or tomatoes, which can't be prepackaged.

There's limited refrigeration aboard the ISS, so foods and beverages are typically kept at room temperature and this means no ice cream. Although they're never piping hot, many MRE foods can be warmed on the craft in a small food warmer.

Astronauts typically eat freeze-dried or thermostabilized foods that are packaged in flexible, disposable pouches designed to prevent harmful microorganisms, air, and moisture from getting into the food. Many of the pouches are flat for convenient storage, and astronauts can eat right out of the pouches with a spoon or fork.

Freeze-dried foods have had all the moisture removed ahead of time, so they need to have water added back at the onboard rehydration station. Examples would be scrambled eggs, potatoes au gratin, shrimp fried rice, rice pilaf, hamburger patties, cream spinach, and powdered beverages.

Thermostabilized foods are preserved by heat processing and can be eaten right out of the package without added water. Examples would be meat loaf, potato soup, split pea soup, chicken with peanut sauce, and pudding.

Some store-bought foods such as granola bars, cookies, candy, nuts, tuna, or salmon are also available for astronauts.

The Packaging Room in the space food lab is where all food items are placed in protective packages to be preserved before being shipped to the spacecraft.

"Most people are intrigued with this room," Takiyah says. "We have on hairnets, lab coats, and face masks. We have on gloves and little booties like ones worn for surgery. You look like you're going into an operation, but you're packaging food. Those are the precautions we take to make sure our astronauts' food is safe."

Bulk food ingredients are stored in a special area. "Everything is kept under lock and key and tracked in our inventory system," Takiyah says.

Meals in Microgravity

Living and working on a spacecraft such as the International Space Station means being in a closed environment of reduced gravity where everything that's not packaged properly or fastened down could easily float away. Eating utensils and foods have special Velcro pieces on them so they can be stuck to trays or walls and stay put. Beverage packages have special straws with locking clamps so bubbles don't escape and float away.

Avoiding crumbs on the craft is paramount because these small particles could float into an astronaut's eye, ear, or nose, or the equipment. Toast, potato chips, and grated parmesan cheese are examples of crumb-laden foods to be avoided. Instead of eating bread, astronauts use lightweight tortillas for foods such as hamburgers, breakfast burritos, and peanut butter and jelly sandwiches.

In microgravity, astronauts often have a muted sense of taste. It's like eating food with a head cold. So spicy foods like shrimp cocktail and condiments like hot sauce are often very popular.

And what about seasonings? One quick shake of salt could send countless particles into every ISS nook and cranny. For this reason, salt and pepper are available in liquid form.

Creating space food is challenging, but Takiyah says it's come a long way from the early days of spaceflight. "Imagine eating tuna salad out of a toothpaste tube, or a grilled cheese sandwich pressed into the shape of a small Lego. It's just not appetizing."

But how do astronauts choose what to eat every day?

"At one point in the program astronauts ate according to a strict menu," she says. "But we've gotten away from that." Today astronauts choose foods from large containers aboard the ISS that contain categories of foods such as meat and fish, beverages, side dishes, breakfast, and desserts. Astronauts can choose whatever they want to eat, and they can even mix foods together for tasty combos such as mac and cheese with chili. The United States provides about half the food aboard the ISS, and international partners, primarily Russia, provide the other half of the foods.

Astronauts also need to eat more calories than is typically required on Earth because they need to exercise to maintain their health and it takes energy to stay upright and not float around in microgravity.

On top of it all, Takiyah says there is also the psychological aspect that goes along with eating. She is very aware that astronauts may miss being at home, seeing loved ones, and having home-cooked meals. In other words, astronauts also need comfort food. She knows that aside from providing nutrition, treats such as brownies or familiar meals are very important for astronauts on an emotional level. "As NASA evolved, the food had to evolve. It had to look like food, taste like food, and feel like food to make sure the astronauts liked it. If you come up with a product that's beautiful and a great concept but no one wants to eat it, it's no good," she says. "We have a tremendous responsibility."

Making food last a long time is also a challenge that's important for longer-lasting space travels such as the Orion mission and the possibility of human missions to the moon or Mars. The high-calorie space bars Takiyah helped develop would be examples of a food that could last a long time in deep space and nourish astronauts.

"We're constantly asked to push the limits," she says. "One of my biggest projects is a shelf life test, where we process some of our foods in different ways and store them at different temperatures and in different types of packaging. The goal is to see if we can make them last five years. It's been our first time testing for that long, and it's been super interesting!"

Takiyah's Favorites

Time of day: I enjoy early mornings because it sets the tone for the rest of my day.

Time of year: New Years is my favorite time of year because everyone is looking forward to new beginnings!

Place on Earth: My favorite place on Earth is Vanuatu because it has an active volcano.

Space food: Meat loaf, because it's the first product I learned to make when I joined the team.

Earth food: Curry chicken. It's delicious!

Song: "Wild Is the Wind" by Nina Simone.

Quote: "Failure is an important part of your growth. . . . Don't be afraid to fail." —Michelle Obama.

Mentors: My coworker Maya Cooper, who taught me to seek understanding in all situations; Dr. Harold McNabb, a professor I had at Iowa State.

Movie: *Independence Day*, because I'm a huge Will Smith fan.

Book: *Me Before You* by Jojo Moyes.

Follow Dr. Takiyah Sirmons Online

Websites: NASA.gov, NASA Space Food: nasa.gov/aero research/resources/artifact-opportunities/space-food/; spacecenter.org

Instagram: @spacecenterhouston; @nasajohnson

Twitter: @NASA

Facebook: @NASA

Sophie Healy-Thow:
Science and Food Activism

Sophie Healy-Thow had been working hard on a food-related science experiment with her teammates Ciara Judge and Émer Hickey. She was naturally surprised when a scientist emailed them saying their concept wouldn't work because it hadn't been done before. "It was a little bit heartbreaking," Sophie says. "But how does he know it won't work if it's never been done before?"

The friends' science project started in 2013 when they were attending Kinsale Community School in Kinsale, Ireland, and decided to enter the BT (British Telecommunications) Young Scientist and Technology science fair in Dublin.

For their experiment they set out to investigate whether the germination rates of various cereal crops could be increased to help combat world hunger. Inspiration for their project blossomed both at school and at home.

In their geography class, Sophie, Ciara, and Émer learned about global food crises and how vital crops sometimes failed early on in their growth. They wondered why this happened and what could be done about it.

One day when Émer was gardening at home with her mom, she discovered that their pea plants had bumpy nodules on their roots. She wondered if there was something wrong with the peas and then asked her teacher about it during biology class. The teacher explained that legumes, such as peas and beans, have small nodules on their roots that hold diazotrophs, which are beneficial bacteria that help them grow.

In addition, Sophie, Ciara, and Émer learned that nonlegume cereal plants such as wheat, oats, and barley do not have these root nodules and are not able to absorb the beneficial diazotroph bacteria. They started to wonder why this occurred and the seed for their science fair project was planted.

Next step? They began to conduct initial research about their topic. It didn't take long to discover that scientists had already tried to place diazotrophs directly on the roots of nonlegume plants to speed up germination rates. However, the teammates learned that this technique didn't seem to work.

They wondered if beneficial bacteria could be applied directly to the seeds of wheat, oats, and barley to speed up the growth process and produce more food in the long run. Now armed with this hypothesis, they got right to work.

Even though some individuals didn't think their concept was viable, they diligently moved forward with their science experiment titled "Combating the Global Food Crisis: Diazotroph Bacteria as a Cereal Growth Promoter."

They then entered their project in various competitions in Ireland, Europe, and the United States, and the results were win-win! In 2013 they won the BT Young Scientists of the Year in Dublin, as well as the European Union Contest for Young Scientists in Prague. In 2014, the three teens won the grand prize in the Google Science Fair in Mountain View, California. They were also selected for *Time* magazine's list of "Top 25 Most Influential Teens" that same year. And Sophie has been influencing and helping others ever since.

Sophie Healy-Thow is an award-winning youth activist who advocates for food security and gender equality in our world. She is a lead group member of the Scaling Up Nutrition (SUN) movement, and the cochair of the youth liaison group of the United Nations Food Systems Summit. In 2020 she was listed by Food Tank as one of 18 inspiring young persons dedicated to changing food systems. She is also a youth leader in Act4Food Act4Change sponsored by the Global Alliance for Improved Nutrition (GAIN), the Food Foundation, the UN Food Systems Summit, Irish Aid, and United Kingdom Aid.

Sophie was born in Cork, Ireland, and grew up in the small fishing town of Kinsale, located in the southern part of the country. Kinsale sits at the mouth of the River Bandon, which flows to the Celtic Sea. She could always see the river, farms, and fields from her home and says she's always had a close connection to the sea and green open spaces. "If I'm away from the sea for too long, I feel claustrophobic."

Sophie's grandmother, Gran, grew up on Heir Island, which is a small island off the southwest coast of Ireland. Heir Island was a place Sophie loved to visit. "It's the most magical place on the planet and is stuck in time when things were simple and beautiful. There are very few cars and no Wi-Fi out there, so you're forced to enjoy the beauty of simplicity."

When Gran met Sophie's grandfather, a fisherman, she moved to Kinsale. Sophie, her mum, and her sister eventually moved two houses down from her Gran. "A lot of my childhood was spent with her and my aunts," Sophie says. "And my earliest memories of food were probably with Gran."

Her grandmother had a plot of land behind her home where she would grow apples, strawberries, and delicious tomatoes that Sophie called "Nana's apples." Sophie loved to eat the fresh produce from the garden and says she's always been "surrounded by a love for food and cooking."

She learned to cook from everyone in her family. Her grandmother would share all her recipes, and her Aunt Helen made a special recipe book for her. Her dad also loved to cook and would often bake banana bread with Sophie and her younger sister, Esha.

From about five to sixteen years old, Sophie and Esha, who were close in age, were very into gymnastics. "I loved, loved,

loved gymnastics, and I was focused on the beam and the bar," Sophie says. She also ran competitively in the 100- and 200-meter sprint and the long jump.

Growing up, Sophie loved reading, sketching, and art history. "I think if I wasn't doing what I do now, I would be studying art history."

Although science brought Sophie into the spotlight during her teens, she admits she wasn't interested in science until she was older. Not only that, school wasn't her cup of tea. "I didn't really enjoy school at all. I found that it was a lot of rote learning and just kind of regurgitating facts."

But things changed when she discovered she could enter science competitions. Suddenly, learning about science became an exciting adventure, and she enjoyed learning from her peers while at science fairs. "Science is all around us, and it's linked to creating and building and learning new things," Sophie says. "Science is linked to the soil, the climate, and even my own body. It really fascinated me."

After Sophie, Ciara, and Émer decided to move forward with their science project on plant growth, they first needed to find seeds. Fortunately, they got free seeds at a local seed store. "But getting the strain of bacteria we wanted was a little bit more tricky," Sophie says.

The teammates contacted the nearby University College Cork (UCC), which turned out to be a huge help. Biologists at the school gave them the bacteria they needed and then showed them important techniques for how to sterilize seeds, apply bacteria, and incubate seeds. "We got to see these big machines they use, and it was really exciting," Sophie says.

But the teens needed to construct their own scientific equipment at home. They worked in Ciara's house and backyard and cleverly used things such as polystyrene fish boxes and toy trains and tracks for their experiment. "It was a really creative and fun process," Sophie adds. Over many months, they investigated different stages in the growth process of their plants by conducting germination experiments, analyzing enzymes, and then growing plants in plastic crates filled with soil.

Overall, the teammates collected more than 100,000 manual measurements of their plants while using control measures for accuracy. Some of the seeds were treated with bacteria, while other seeds were treated with water. After many months of working on their science experiment, they did find increases in the germination rates of some of the crops. "The experiment worked best on barley and oats and didn't work as well on wheat," Sophie says.

Attending the 2014 Google Science Fair in California was the first time Sophie had ever been in the United States. "Everything was so big and colorful and lit up all the time. I remember seeing the self-driving cars and everybody was just so nice."

Being at Google was a huge awakening for Sophie, especially when she talked with young people who visited their exhibit. "I was explaining how our project was about growing crops at a faster rate, which meant that less water was needed and less time for harvest. I explained how this was needed in areas where they experience drought and food insecurity—but I was met with blank faces. It really hit me that this needs to be talked about."

Food Insecurity and Hunger

Millions of people around the world struggle with food insecurity and hunger. As defined by the Food and Agriculture Organization of the United Nations, "A person is food insecure when they lack regular access to enough safe and nutritious food for normal growth and development and an active and healthy life. This may be due to unavailability of food and/or lack of resources to obtain food."

Examples of food insecurity would be when a person doesn't have enough money to buy food, doesn't have transportation to get to a food store, doesn't have nutritious food in their community, and doesn't have adequate health care.

According to the Food and Agriculture Organization of the United Nations, food insecurity can be experienced at different levels of severity from mild to severe.

People who are food insecure often experience hunger, which is an uncomfortable or painful feeling in the body when they don't have enough food or water. Hunger is often referred to as "undernourishment."

Issues around food insecurity and hunger are complex, and there are many people and organizations worldwide working hard to combat these ongoing problems. The goal is that every human being is food secure with the proper nutrition to grow and thrive.

A big part of Sophie Healy-Thow's work is to help reduce food insecurity and hunger in our world. For more information, check out www.un.org/en/global-issues/food.

At that moment, Sophie knew exactly what she wanted to do with her life. She wanted to reach out to young people to bring awareness to global food and hunger issues.

She was still in secondary school at the time and was suddenly bombarded with requests to attend conferences around the world. Sophie was often the only young person in the room and didn't like attending the conferences. "I was grateful to be included and invited," she says. "But I was often given a space to talk but not really heard. This was always quite disappointing."

Fortunately, she was not deterred, and she cleverly used social media to speak up. "I had just started tweeting, and I gained this new confidence in not being afraid to say what I thought."

World Food Day

Every year on October 16, people from around the world recognize and celebrate World Food Day (WFD). This international day shines much-needed light on the devastation of hunger, food insecurity, and malnutrition on our planet. World Food Day commemorates the Food and Agriculture Organization (FAO) of the United Nations, which was founded October 16, 1945.

According to the FAO, "More than 3 billion people (almost 40% of the world's population) cannot afford a healthy diet."

World Food Day gives people ideas about ways to take action to combat and eradicate these global problems. Examples of ways to get involved include choosing healthy diets and sustainable food, helping reduce food waste, composting foods, supporting small food producers, finding ways to make nutritious foods available and affordable, and getting the word out about hunger and malnutrition.

Every year WFD has a theme, starting in 1981 with "Food Comes First." Examples of World Food Day themes from the past six years include:

- 2016: "Climate Is Changing. Food and Agriculture Must Too."
- 2017: "Change the Future of Migration. Invest in Food Security and Rural Development."
- 2018: "Our Actions Are Our Future. A #ZeroHunger World by 2030 Is Possible."
- 2019: "Our Actions Are Our Future. Healthy Diets for a #ZeroHunger World."
- 2020: "Grow, Nourish, Sustain. Together. Our Actions Are Our Future."
- 2021: "Safe Food Now for a Healthy Tomorrow."

For more information, check out www.fao.org/world-food-day/en.

In 2015 Sophie got a direct message on Twitter from the United Nations and wondered if she was being pranked. But the message was real, and Sophie was invited to attend the United Nations' launch of the Sustainable Development Goals in New York City. Sophie was prepared to talk about "Sustainable Development Goal 2: Zero Hunger" and why young people need to be involved. Although she was unable to speak due to time constraints, it was a still a huge learning experience.

"I was painfully shy growing up," Sophie says. "But stepping out of my comfort zone and speaking to people about things I'm passionate about was one of the best things I could have done for myself. I'm naturally an introvert, but when you find that one thing you love and you're passionate about it, it will crack your shell and you'll be thankful for it in the end."

Her life was opening up big time. In her final year of secondary school she became a volunteer board member with the nonprofit ActionAid United Kingdom. "It's the first place I felt included and listened to at a level where decisions were being made. It made me realize that young people should be at the decision-making table." ActionAid UK also invited her to visit Rwanda where she got to see the amazing work of farmers—especially women farmers.

In 2017 Sophie began attending University College Cork to study international development and food policy. The university wasn't far from home, and she had inspiring courses in gender studies, the history of agriculture, economics, politics, and community building.

One of her most unforgettable lectures was about architect Buckminster Fuller's famous "Spaceship Earth" essay on Earth's limited resources. "It was about how we're all floating around on a big rock like a spaceship," she says. "If our population continues to grow, we're not going to have anything left, so we need to start rethinking the way we use our resources. It's so simple, but it makes so much sense."

In her gender studies courses Sophie learned about the changing role of women in the global food industry, which was a real eye-opener. "I was like, hang on, where do women fit in here and where do they fit in the food systems?" She wanted to learn more.

Attending University College Cork was exciting, but it was also a very difficult and painful time. "My dad passed away when I was in my first year," Sophie says. Thankfully, the women in her family were there for her. "I've always had strong female influences, and my mom is my role model. I realized how strong females are and how much of the weight of the world they have on their shoulders."

Despite her family struggles, Sophie kept going. She volunteered for a youth organization in Ireland called One Campaign that strives to end poverty, and she met many young people who wanted to create change in the world. In 2017 she traveled to Brussels, Belgium, to participate in the Youth Agriculture Summit.

And much to her joy, Sophie had a paid UCC internship with the Concern Worldwide organization. "I made a podcast called *Midday Snackbox*, which I loved doing," she says. Today, Sophie is very involved as a youth leader with the Act-4Food Act4Change campaigns that began in May 2021. "Every single decision that's made by Act4Food Act4Change is made by a young person," Sophie says. "Our youngest member is 15, and our oldest is 28 years."

Act4Change involves many youth leaders from all over the world in efforts to change and improve global food systems through innovative programs and workshops. "These young people are like a whole other force of nature," Sophie says. "They're amazing!"

Sophie joined forces with Kenyan nutritionist and Act4Food Act4Change leader, Maureen Muketha, to write an Act4Food pledge designed to bring young people together "to mobilise and influence tangible, positive change in our world's food systems."

The Act4Food Pledge

We know our current food systems contribute to ongoing health, climate and biodiversity crises, and violation of human rights. We will only be able to achieve the United Nations Sustainable Development Goals with a fundamental transformation of our food systems.

While we as young people have been excluded from most political and economic decision-making processes, we are also the ones who will live the longest with the consequences of decisions made today.

We pledge to act. And we demand urgent large-scale action from others, especially from decision-makers in government and business.

As youth we #Act4Food #Act4Change to support #GoodFoodForAll

For more information, check out https://actions4food.org/en/https://actions4food.org/en/.

From working with tiny diazotrophs in her early teens to gigantic global organizations today, Sophie Healy-Thow is determined to help change and improve our world. "Everybody has something that they've gone through that brings them here today and has made them so passionate about what we're doing," she says. "You have to be quite an optimistic person because we're met with so many different obstacles. The community is so important, and I'm so lucky to always come back to strong female role models."

Sophie's Favorites

Time of day: Morning around 7:00 AM. The house is quiet, and I have my first cup of coffee. I open the back door and sit on the step to enjoy the fresh air of a new day!

Time of year: Christmas. The whole family comes together, and we eat good food and laugh and spend quality time together.

Place on Earth: Heir Island. This is the little island where my grandmother, Gran, grew up.

Food: My gran's famous apple pie. If you tried it, you'd understand why. She used to make it with her own apples from her garden.

Mentor: My mum.

Song: "People Have Names" by Juliet Turner.

Sayings: "Listen quietly, listen with intent, and listen with understanding," by Stephen Covey from his book, *The 7 Habits of Highly Effective People*.

Movie: *Spirited Away*.

Book: I have a lot of favorite books, but my newest favorite is *Girl Woman Other* by Bernardine Evaristo.

Follow Sophie Healy-Thow Online

Website: https://actions4food.org/en/; https://actions 4change.org

Instagram: @sophiehealythow

Twitter: @SophieHealyThow

Facebook: Sophie Healy-Thow

Dr. Pia Sörensen: Science and Cooking

When Pia Sörensen presents the popular topic of fermentation in her science and cooking courses, her students often bubble over with excitement. It all has to do with their hands-on sauerkraut assignment.

To show how fermentation works, specifically lacto-fermentation, Pia has students chop up green or purple cabbage into thin strips in the on-campus lab. They then add the proportionate percent of salt and knead the cabbage in a large bowl to release its water and reduce its size. The salt, via osmosis, draws the water out of the cabbage. Then the briny concoction is tightly packed into a glass jar with a lid. Students label and date their fermentation jars.

The scientific process has begun.

Students take their jars home to observe what happens when microbes on the cabbage start to transform the food over the next few weeks. They'll taste small amounts from the jar to notice how the flavor changes. They'll observe how the color changes and watch what happens inside the jar. Sometimes it's dramatic. "Students notice that the cabbage gets more sour over time," Pia says. "This is a lactic-acid fermentation, so it produces lactic acid, which makes it acidic."

And because the fermentation process produces carbon dioxide, the cabbage mixture will usually start to bubble, depending on variables such as room temperature. Pia says that this is when she sometimes hears from students. "I'll get these emails that say, 'I don't know what to do! The jar is bubbling and flowing over and I have purple cabbage juice all over. It's ALIVE!'" she laughs. "But I love this. Of course it's alive because you're cooking with a living organism. You can't fully understand it by reading about it in a book. You have to do it."

Pia Sörensen teaches Flavor Molecules of Food Fermentation: Exploration and Inquiry, and coteaches Science and Cooking: From Haute Cuisine to Soft Matter Science at the Harvard John A. Paulson School of Engineering and Applied Sciences in Boston, Massachusetts. Pia is also coauthor (with Michael Brenner and David Weitz) of *Science and Cooking: Physics Meets Food, from Homemade to Haute Cuisine,* published in 2020. She has a PhD in chemical biology from Harvard, and a BS in molecular biophysics and biochemistry from Yale.

Pia grew up in the province of Scania in southern Sweden. As a young person she was very connected to science and nature and spent her days exploring the woods and fields of her town. She was also very active in scouting. "I loved the outdoors—sleeping in tents, going hiking, and trying to live off of what you could find in the forest."

She also enjoyed staying with her maternal grandparents in their summer cottage. "My grandparents had a little cottage in the middle of the forest next to a small lake." Pia loved to swim in the lake. She also had ample room to explore the plants, flowers, birds, and trees of the region. "At the lake there were these small flowers called *nattviol*, and their smell would only come out at night," she says. "We would go out at dusk and smell them."

She says these tiny white flowers (*Platanthera bifolia*) are related to the orchid family and she was absolutely mesmerized by their strong fragrance. Her grandfather would carefully protect the delicate flowers with wooden sticks so no one would step on them.

Pia's main interest in nature as a child was through botany, and she liked to paint pictures of flowers with watercolors. She and her grandmother would also collect and press many flowers and herbs. "I had my own herbarium that I collected," she says. "I could sit for hours with a botany book and look through it. I knew the names of all the flowers in Swedish and also some in Latin. I was fascinated by the sheer beauty of looking really closely at nature."

All throughout school, Pia enjoyed taking many science classes. She says that her mom, who was an engineer, encouraged her to have an interest in math as well as the natural sciences, such as physics, chemistry, and biology.

Her introduction to food was a very positive one, and she always had family meals with her parents and younger siblings. "Food was a big thing," she says. "The women in my family were fantastic cooks, and I should give my grandfather some credit because he cooked amazing pancakes."

Her mother baked a lot of bread from scratch and would often make delicious fruit compotes for dessert. Her family would stock up on chickens from her aunt and uncle's farm, and she also loved eating her grandmother's Swedish meatballs and potatoes.

But there were some food challenges. "I was a very picky eater," she says. "I remember sitting with a piece of fish where some grown-up had convinced me there were no bones in the fish. And of course I would find bones. But I'm not nearly as picky now as I used to be."

After graduating from high school, she took two years off to explore the world. "This is something I highly recommend," she says. Pia spent time in Greece doing research for Archelon, a nonprofit organization that protects sea turtles and their habitats. From Greece she traveled to Germany to study literature and philosophy. And then it was on to England where she immersed herself in liberal arts and the humanities while working in restaurants to pay the rent.

These experiences, which Pia calls her wanderings, helped solidify that, although she liked the humanities, she was most interested in the sciences.

Next it was on to the Bay Area of California where she became a chemistry major at the University of California, Berkeley. She says that as someone who's very interested in the natural world and the plants and animals around her, Pia immediately noticed that the Bay Area had a very different environment from Sweden. "It's really more like a Mediterranean climate, and the entire flora and fauna are different. I didn't know the names of anything, and it was very much a feeling of being in a different place. I would walk outside on one of my first days and just smell the spices in the air and the minty smell of the eucalyptus trees."

After studying at Berkeley, Pia transferred to Yale University in New Haven, Connecticut, where she continued her studies and graduated with a bachelor of science degree.

Next, she moved to Cambridge, Massachusetts, where she earned her PhD in chemical biology at Harvard.

Something magical happened for her at this important time in her life. She began to teach while working on her doctoral degree, and it was a huge aha moment. "I loved teaching during my PhD," she says. "It was my favorite part. So I was looking for creative ways that I could teach science and have it as a job."

Pia learned that professors Michael Brenner and David Weitz had just started a new course called Science and Cooking at Harvard in 2010. The goal of Science and Cooking is to teach physics, chemistry, and a little bit of biology through food. In 2011 Pia came onboard to help teach the class. "I've been doing it ever since," she says. "We often describe our team by saying that Michael is the mathematician, Dave is the physicist, and I'm the chemist and biologist."

The course is open to all students who are nonscience majors wanting to fulfill their science requirements. The class is presented in a large lecture hall on campus with a separate cooking lab. Depending on enrollment there are between 100 to 350 students who take the class.

During the lab portion of the class, students make various foods to better understand the underlying science. And depending on what they make, they can literally gobble up their experiments. The class is also taught online via HarvardX where students around the world conduct their food experiments in their kitchens at home.

A number of the students are surprised by the course's focus on science and math. "Some students go into the course thinking this is going to be all about cooking," Pia says. "They may not realize that this is real hard-core science. It's soft matter physics. It's physical chemistry. It's not a cooking course, it's a science course."

Each week of the course has a unique theme. Heady concepts such as heat transfer, diffusion, phase transitions, and fermentation come to life as students begin recognizing the science behind how we cook and bake. Students learn that recipes are like scientific formulas in that food ingredients need to be mathematically measured and weighed—and temperature causes the underlying molecular transformations when materials like water go from a solid (ice), to a liquid (glass of water), to a gas (steam).

After Pia had been coteaching the class for almost 10 years, she, Michael Brenner, and David Weitz published their *Science and Cooking: Physics Meets Food, from Homemade to Haute Cuisine* book in 2020. The book, which is used in the classroom and online, is chock-full of scientific recipes to make chocolate chip cookies, filo pastry, almond pralines, ice cream, ceviche, poached eggs, and caramelized carrot soup, to name a few. Readers learn a great deal about the sweet and savory science behind cooking and baking. Examples include the texture molecules of proteins, fats, and carbohydrates and the flavor molecules of sweet, sour, salty, bitter, and umami.

What Is Flavor?

A sweet watermelon-flavored sorbet. A savory slice of pizza. A salty pretzel. Each of these foods tempts our taste buds with a different kind of flavor. But how do we experience flavor?

Eating is a sensory process. "Every food contains exceptionally small flavor molecules that are detected by the taste buds on our tongues and the olfactory receptors in our noses," Pia says. "The tastes of sweet, sour, salty, bitter, and umami are detected on the tongue, while others, like vanilla, clove, and basil, are detected in our noses."

The overall sensation from our taste buds and our olfactory receptors is collectively referred to as flavor. Our other senses of vision, hearing, and touch also play a role. All of this sensory input gets wired through the brain to send us messages about the flavor of what we're eating. Yum!

One of the most exciting parts of the Science and Cooking class is having chefs come in to share their knowledge and expertise. One such chef is Joanne Chang, who owns the popular Flour Bakery + Cafe in Cambridge and Boston. Joanne has earned many James Beard Award nominations plus a James Beard win for Outstanding Baker in 2016. "Joanne was an applied math major at Harvard and then she decided to go into baking. Her Flour Bakery is sort of a Boston establishment," Pia says. "She comes and talks about the science of sugar. She does such a good job explaining the many different roles of sugar in sweets. We've invited her back every year for the last 10 years."

Spanish chef and restaurateur, José Andrés, who founded the World Central Kitchen, which provides nutritious food to individuals impacted by disasters, has also presented a number of lectures for the class over the years. His presentations are often about diffusion and gelling agents.

In the fall of 2021, James Beard Award–nominated chef Amanda Cohen came in to talk about veggies with a flavorful lecture titled "Fooling the Eye, Tricking the Tongue: Breaking Flavor Associations with Vegetables." Amanda owns the award-winning vegetable restaurant Dirt Candy in New York

City. "Dirt Candy was the first vegetable-focused restaurant in the city and is a pioneer of the vegetable-forward movement."

Also in 2021, Atlanta barbecue chef Bryan Furman gave an unforgettable presentation on barbecue. "We moved the class outside for that day and pitmaster Bryan smoked barbecue ribs in a huge smoker starting at seven in the morning," Pia says. "Everyone got to taste the ribs at the end of class, and we talked about the science of heat transfer and calculated the diffusion coefficient of smoke from the smoke ring."

What Are Fermented Foods and Beverages?

Fermented foods are part of most traditional diets around the world. "Many of us eat them every day, often without knowing how they are made or that they may have been produced with yeast or even bacteria, which we often shun as having to do with disease and bad hygiene." But the microscopic yeast or bacterial microbes that help create fermented foods are different. These microbes help bring to life a wide range of fermented foods and beverages to create a chemical change in flavor, texture, and nutritional value. For example, bacteria convert cabbage into lactic acid to create sauerkraut. Sourdough bread is made when bacteria produce lactic acid and yeast produces carbon dioxide in a mixture of flour and water. Other examples of fermented foods and beverages include: chocolate, cheese, yogurt, kimchi, gherkins, miso, tempeh, apple cider vinegar, kefir, kombucha tea, wine, and beer.

Pia realized that fermentation was becoming a hot topic in food. She noticed that fine-dining chefs were starting to incorporate fermented foods into their menus and people were making fermented foods at home. So she designed her own course on fermentation, which began in 2015. "A lot of chemists and biologists take this course," she says about this smaller research-based class designed for science majors.

Although her day-to-day life is very food focused in her science and cooking classes, she still enjoys cooking at home. "I have a saffron and fish soup I love to cook and I have a big thing for potatoes. I'm also hugely into sweets."

But sometimes her classwork impacts her desire to cook at home. "We have an entire lab on making mayonnaise," she says. "If you walk into the lab that week, it just smells of garlic and mustard, and I probably would not go home that week and make mayonnaise. We also have a lab on lava cake, molten chocolate cake, and that week the lab smells amazing but after a week of that I probably would not go home and make chocolate cake."

Science can be intimidating for students, and Pia says that teaching the basic principles of science through cooking can be helpful. "I think all of us have some kind of human desire to understand the world around us. And it doesn't matter if that's the plant in your garden or the food you cook in the kitchen or a fascination with the night sky," Pia says. "So, what I try to do is figure out if there are specific things in people that they're especially curious about. And then use that to explore the science. And my big thing is that I do it with food. There is so much science in food. You can teach almost any subject with food."

There's a lot that Pia loves about her work. "I love that I get to be curious about the world around me. And I love that I get to interact with the students and other curious people and that we can be curious together."

Pia's Favorites

Time of day: Dusk because of the golden light.

Time of year: I like most times of the year for so many reasons. But I definitely like summer because of swimming and winter because of skiing.

Place on Earth: A lake in southern Sweden.

Food to discuss: Sauerkraut.

Food to cook: Everything with potatoes.

Food to eat: My grandmother's meatballs.

Follow Dr. Pia Sörensen Online

Websites: sorensen.seas.harvard.edu; sciencecooking .seas.harvard.edu

Instagram: @scicookharvard

Twitter: @SciCook

Afterword

Seed farmer Petra Page-Mann says that "seeds are living links in this long line of everything that has been and everything that will be." She even calls seeds "beautiful love letters from the past."

It's so true. Seeds are amazing blueprints for life and the beginning of something new.

For farmers like Petra and many people who find fulfilling careers in the food industry, it all begins with the tiny bundle of potential energy called a seed. This could be the seed of a food, such as a tomato, apple, or pomegranate. Or it could be the seed of one's own imagination that brings forth exciting adventures and challenges. But it all starts somewhere.

There are so many unique opportunities in the food industry, and finding the right fit for you is key. Would you like to work the soil and be a farmer who enjoys producing crops in the fresh air? How about studying chemistry, physics, and biology to become a food scientist? Perhaps you'd like to find a niche in the kitchen and delight people with amazing delicacies and dishes. Or you might use your talent with writing and photography to shed light on important food matters. Just think about it.

Life paths often take many directions, and they can easily zigzag along. A number of the women featured in this book started on one path and then found joy in a completely different direction.

For example, Tracy Obolsky started out as an artist and then became an amazing pastry chef and business owner. Gail Taylor used her skills in politics and social justice to become an urban farmer. Cheetie Kumar found her voice and talents onstage as well as in the kitchen.

In addition, many of the women have had multiple roles in their careers that require different kinds of creativity and skill sets. You've read about podcaster Andi Murphy who also loves to cook, food activist Haleh Zandi who enjoys farming, and cookbook author Jocelyn Ramirez who is a chef and businesswoman.

From farmers and chefs to food activists, storytellers, and food scientists, all of the women in this book have similar characteristics that vibrantly shine throughout their stories. They all have the willingness to learn about their areas of expertise, the desire to follow their personal passions and dreams, the strength to take risks, the ability to be of service, and the fortitude to succeed and find happiness.

Now, what will *you* plant and grow for your own life?

Acknowledgments

I'd like to thank the 15 women in this book who were open to being interviewed so they could share their amazing stories. They all lead very busy lives, and I truly appreciated the time they gave me to help create this book about women in the food industry. I'd also like to thank my Chicago Review Press editor, Jerome Pohlen, for his kindness and patience throughout the writing process. I'm grateful for the input from Josh Madeira and Sheila Bowman with the Monterey Bay Aquarium in Monterey, California, and Karen Hsueh with the Insight Garden Program in Berkeley, California. Last, I'd also like to thank all the good eggs who helped with excellent editorial input along the way.

Notes

Chapter 1: Emma de Long

"Five bald eagles": All quotes from original author interviews with Emma de Long on November 23 and November 24, 2020, unless otherwise noted here.

"worldwide movement": "About WWOOF: Mission," Federation of WWOOF Organisation, https://wwoof.net/fowo/.

The concept of: Jennifer Ross, "The Origins of Community Supported Agriculture (CSA)," March 7, 2019, https://heartbeetfarms.com /who-invented-community-supported-agriculture-csa/.

"Its framework is": Rohini Walker, "The Indigenous Science of Permaculture," December 23 2019, https://www.kcet.org/shows/tending -nature/the-indigenous-science-of-permaculture.

Chapter 2: Gail Taylor

"It's when people": All quotes are from original author interview with Gail Taylor on February 6, 2021, unless otherwise noted here.

"Food security, as defined": "Food Security," International Food Policy Research Institute, https://www.ifpri.org/topic/food-security.

"Young black farmers": Gail Taylor, "Three Part Harmony Farm Logo," February 11, 2014, http://threepartharmonyfarm.org/about-the-three -part-harmony-farm-logo/.

Chapter 3: Petra Page-Mann

"I would be in the mountains": All quotes are from original author interview with Petra Page-Mann on December 15, 2020, unless otherwise noted here.

In the summer of 1858: Brian Mann, "Retracing Ralph Waldo Emerson's Steps in a Now 'Unchanged Eden,'" NPR, *All Things Considered*, transcript and recording, July 24, 2015, https://www.npr.org/2015/07/24/425321179 /retracing-ralph-waldo-emersons-steps-in-a-now-unchanged-eden.

"Their tininess contains": Petra Page-Mann, "The Anatomy of a Seed," *Rise & Shine: Starting Seeds with Ease*, https://www.fruitionseeds .com/wp-content/uploads/Rise-Shine-2021.pdf.

"If you have come here": Lilla Watson, "The Origin of 'Our Liberty is Bound Together,'" Invisible Children, https://invisiblechildren.com /blog/2012/04/04/the-origin-of-our-liberty-is-bound-together/.

Chapter 4: Caroline Glover

"I sat down with my parents": All quotes are from original author interview with Caroline Glover on March 2, 2021, and March 6, 2021, unless otherwise noted here.

"When the going": Glynn Wilson, "When the Going Gets Weird, the Weird Turn Pro," *New American Journal*, March 28, 2019, https://www .newamericanjournal.net/2019/03/when-the-going-gets-weird-the -weird-turn-pro/.

Chapter 5: Cheetie Kumar

"I imagined a cushy": All quotes are from original author interview with Cheetie Kumar on August 16, 2021, unless otherwise noted here.

"I recognized the culture": "About Chefs: Cheetie Kumar Raleigh, NC," Brown in the South, https://www.browninthesouth.com.

Money earned from: "Our Mission," Southern Foodways Alliance, https:// www.southernfoodways.org/about-us/.

Chapter 6: Tracy Obolsky

"The snowstorm was a doozy": All quotes are from original author interview with Tracy Obolsky on September 21, 2021, unless otherwise noted here.

"Dream as if": Karen Clemens Warrick, *James Dean: Dream As If You'll Live Forever*, (Berkeley Heights, NJ: Enslow Publishing LLC, 2006).

Chapter 7: Dani Nierenberg

"It was a very open-air": All quotes from original author interview with Danielle Nierenberg on December 8, 2020, unless otherwise noted here.

"In Kibera, Nairobi": Danielle Nierenberg and Bernard Pollack, Worldwatch Institute, "Nourishing the Planet," posted by Jeffrey A. Brez, March 22, 2011, https://ifad-un.blogspot.com/2011/03/nourishing-planet.html.

"As a global thought leader": "The Julia Child Award Recipient for 2020—Danielle Nierenberg," https://juliachildaward.com/recipients/danielle-nierenberg/.

"At the close of 1942": Dr. Kelly A. Spring, "Julia Child (1912–2004)," National Women's History Museum, 2017, https://www.womenshistory.org/education-resources/biographies/julia-child.

Chapter 8: Haleh Zandi

"I had to go through": All quotes are from original author interview with Haleh Zandi on July 19, 2021.

Chapter 9: Sheila Lucero

"The Blue Ribbon Task Force": All quotes are from original author interview with Sheila Lucero on September 2, 2021, unless otherwise noted here.

"The Magnuson-Stevens": "NOAA Fisheries, Laws & Policies, Magnuson-Stevens Act," https://www.fisheries.noaa.gov/topic/laws-policies.

"As chefs, we are": "ACT Sign the Portland Pact for Sustainable Seafood," https://www.chefsforfish.org/act/.

Chapter 10: Andi Murphy

"Okay, cool. That sounds": All quotes are from original author interview with Andi Murphy on January 22, 2021, unless otherwise noted here.

"Generally, Indigenous*"*: "Native American and Indigenous Peoples FAQs," UCLA Equity, Diversity & Inclusion, updated April 14, 2020, https:// equity.ucla.edu/know/resources-on-native-american-and-indigenous -affairs/native-american-and-indigenous-peoples-faqs/#term.

"Food sovereignty is the right": "Food Sovereignty," US Food Sovereignty Alliance, http://usfoodsovereigntyalliance.org/what-is-food -sovereignty/.

"Food sovereignty is reclaiming": Kerry Diamond and Andi Murphy, "Native American Voices in Food with Toasted Sister's Andi Murphy," *Radio Cherry Bombe,* podcast, EP303, November 2, 2020, https:// cherrybombe.com/radio-cherry-bombe/toasted-sister-andi-murphy.

Chapter 11: Abby Fuller

"I'd heard about Slovenia": All quotes are from original author interview with Abby Fuller on October 6, 2021.

Chapter 12: Jocelyn Ramirez

"I had already been": All quotes are from original author interviews with Jocelyn Ramirez on March 24 and April 30, 2021, unless otherwise noted here.

"The language we use": Nina Sevilla, "Food Apartheid: Racialized Access to Healthy Affordable Food," Natural Resources Defense Council (NRDC), April 2, 2021, https://www.nrdc.org/experts/nina-sevilla /food-apartheid-racialized-access-healthy-affordable-food.

Chapter 13: Dr. Takiyah Sirmons

"This was my first NASA": All quotes are from original author interview with Dr. Takiyah Sirmons on January 27, 2021, unless otherwise noted here.

"Failure is an important": Celia Fernandez, "34 Michelle Obama Quotes That Will Inspire You to Live Your Best Life," Oprah Daily, February 9, 2022, https://www.oprahdaily.com/life/relationships-love/g25438427/michelle-obama-quotes/.

Chapter 14: Sophie Healy-Thow

"It was a little bit": All quotes are from original author interview with Sophie Healy-Thow on October 19, 2021, unless otherwise noted here.

"A person is food insecure": "Hunger and Food Insecurity," Food and Agriculture Organization of the United Nations, https://www.fao.org/hunger/en/.

People who are: "Hunger and Food Insecurity," Food and Agriculture Organization of the United Nations, https://www.fao.org/hunger/en/.

"More than 3 billion people": "World Food Day 16 October 2021," Food and Agriculture Organization of the United Nations, https://www.fao.org/world-food-day/about/en.

"to mobilise and influence": ACT4FOOD, https://actions4food.org/en/.

"We know our current": "Make Your Pledge Today," ACT4FOOD, https://actions4food.org/en/.

Chapter 15: Dr. Pia Sörensen

"Students notice that": All quotes are from original author interview with Dr. Pia Sörensen on October 15, 2021, unless otherwise noted here.

"Dirt Candy was the first": "Chef," Dirt Candy, https://www.dirtcandynyc.com/chef.

"Many of us eat": David Weitz, Michael Brenner, and Pia Sörensen, *Science and Cooking: Physics Meets Food, From Homemade to Haute Cuisine*, (New York: W.W. Norton & Company, 2020), 240.